THUNDERBOLT
AND LIGHTNING

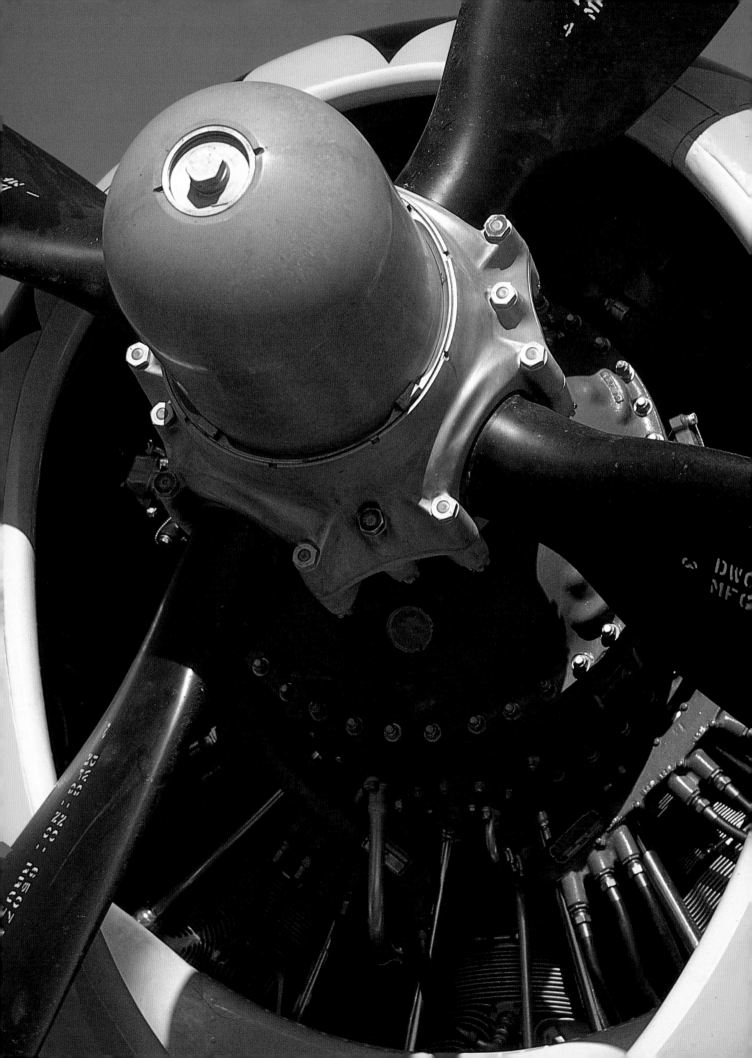

THUNDERBOLT AND LIGHTNING

THE JUG AND THE FORK-TAILED DEVIL

MICHAEL O'LEARY

First published in Great Britain in 1996

by Osprey, an imprint of Reed Consumer Books Limited

Michelin House, 81 Fulham Road,London SW3 6RB

and Auckland, Melbourne, Singapore and Toronto

© 1996 Osprey Publishing

ISBN 1 85532519 5

Edited by Tony Holmes
Design by Paul Kime

Printed in Hong Kong

HALF TITLE PAGE *Detail view of the artwork for BIG CHIEF, alias P-47D NX47RP, as the cowling sits on the Chino ramp while the R-2800 receives a check up*

TITLE PAGE *Motive power for the Thunderbolt. One of the most effective and most produced aero engines of World War 2 was the Pratt & Whitney (P&W) R-2800. Formed in 1925, the company quickly become well-known in the aviation community for its powerful radial engines. Work on the P&W R-2800, named Double Wasp, began in 1936. Designed with 18 cylinders and displacing 2804 cubic inches, the engine was created for a military demanding more and more power for the new generation of bombers and fighters on the drawing boards. Flying somewhat in the face of liquid-cooled V-12s that offered high horsepower combined with lower frontal area, the company forged ahead with the R-2800, and in nine months had the engine running at 2000 hp. An early variant of the engine was fitted to the prototype Vought XF4U-1, which set a level speed record of 405 mph, and orders for the powerplant came flooding in from both Britain and America. The R-2800 would go on to become one of the most produced military and civilian radial engines in history*

RIGHT *The sound of two R-2800s rumbles through the mountains of southern California as John Maloney flies formation on the camera aircraft in Curtiss-built P-47G USAAF s/n 42-25234 NX3395G while Steve Hinton maintains the wingman position in P-47D USAAF s/n 45-49205/NX47RP during July 1986*

Contents

RIGHT *A pair of Allison V-1710s keep Ronnie Gardner aloft as he holds P-38M-6-LO USAAF s/n 44-53095/NX9005R almost directly over Howard Pardue's T-6 camera-ship near Breckenridge, Texas, on 25 March 1991. The aircraft belongs to the Lone Star Flight Museum in Galveston, Texas, and as with the rest of the museum's operational aircraft, is a superb restoration. One interesting point is the slight 'droop' to the nose gear door, a common affliction of the P-38*

Introduction

During the 1990s, two of the most requested former military aircraft to appear at airshows are the Republic P-47 Thunderbolt and Lockheed P-38 Lightning. Unlike the North American P-51 Mustang, numerous examples of which survived to go on the civil register, the Lightning and Thunderbolt were almost rendered extinct by the end of World War 2.

With the jet age fast approaching, the USAAF (to become the USAF in 1947) had little need for the twin-engined P-38 (costly to maintain and operate) or the big P-47 (newer jets like the Republic P-84 Thunderjet were aimed at performing the fighter-bomber role), so most examples were scrapped. Quite a few Thunderbolts were sent to Latin America to equip Third World air forces, while a few Lightnings soldiered on as high-altitude civil mapping platforms. It is from these sources that most of today's surviving aircraft come.

As warbirds – today's generic term for retired and restored military aircraft – became more popular during the early 1970s, the high-value and most in-demand aircraft was the Mustang. However, this began to change as collectors started to appreciate the rarity of the Thunderbolt and Lightning.

This book is not an attempt to present every surviving P-47 and P-38. Rather, it is a look at some of the aircraft I have photographed over the years, along with historical notes which, hopefully, the reader will find interesting. The intent is to illustrate and document just how these aircraft managed to survive, often in the most haphazard manner, over the years to become today's honoured and revered warbirds.

Michael O'Leary

Los Angeles, California, December 1995

ABOVE *America's oldest privately-owned aviation museum is The Air Museum at Chino, California. During the early 1950s, founder Ed Maloney began collecting the aircraft that nobody wanted, from vintage fabric biplanes that had been eclipsed by the newer all-metal lightplanes, to discarded captured aircraft that had gone through American military evaluation before being unceremoniously dumped as having no further value. Maloney was able to save two Mitsubishi Zero fighters that the US Navy was going to scrap. One aircraft already had its wings cut off in preparation for melt down but the second airframe was relatively complete. The latter was A6M5 61-120, which had been captured by the Allies at Saipan on 18 June 1944 and shipped back to San Diego for evaluation.*

The aircraft was made airworthy and visited several naval installations for testing, logging approximately 190 hours in the hands of American pilots. Maloney originally displayed the non-airworthy Zero at his small museum in Claremont, California, before being moved to several other locations prior to The Air Museum making its permanent home at Chino. In the mid-1970s the decision was made to restore the Zero back to

flying condition – no small task since the inferior metal utilised by the Japanese for the wing spars and become completely corroded and new spars had to be built from scratch. Maloney and his crew dug into the airframe and into the rare Sakae radial engine and, after the expenditure of much money and thousands on man hours, the Zero, now carrying the civil registration N46770, made its first post-restoration flight on 28 June 1978.

It was then despatched on periodic grand tours of Japan, the latest trip occuring in the summer of 1995 in company with a P-51D Mustang, which allowed mock dogfights to be flown for the hundreds of thousands who flocked to see the wartime protagonists.

In our photograph, taken on 20 March 1993, the Zero flies wing on P-38J-20-LO USAAF s/n 44-23314/NX38BP over Lake Matthews near Chino Airport. This unique portrait illustrates the vastly different design philosophies embodied by two of the War's most important combat aircraft. Here, the Zero is being flown by John Maloney, while the P-38 was under the command of Steve Hinton – one would be hard-pressed to find two pilots more skilled in the operation of their respective fighter aircraft

Out to Pasture

LEFT When the 'warbird' movement – defined as the restoration back to flying condition of former World War 2 military aircraft – began in earnest during the late 1960s, the most valuable aircraft to have was the North American P-51D Mustang. This was primarily because the Mustang was the most numerous surviving fighter of the period. The cockpit could also be modified to take a second seat behind the pilot, while engine and airframe spares were readily available. At this time a 'good' Mustang could be obtained for $12,000 to $15,000. All other surviving fighters existed in much fewer numbers than the P-51D, especially the uniquely-configured Lockheed P-38 Lightning.

The fact that even a few P-38s survived was due to their demand as a racing aircraft in the postwar Cleveland National Air Races, and also for their use as a high-altitude photo-mapping platform. However, by the late 1960s, the Cleveland races were long past and newer equipment had gained ascendancy in the photo mapping role. Thus, on 13 November 1967, the rather amazing sight of six sad-looking Lightnings would have greeted a visitor to Santa Barbara Airport in California. The aircraft were parked in front of buildings once occupied by Mark Hurd Aerial Surveys, and had been utilised for a variety of missions before being 'put out to pasture' in favour of new equipment that included a Lear Jet. Three of the Lightnings, each modified to a different standard, are seen in this view

LEFT One of the semi-abandoned Lightnings at Santa Barbara was F-5G-6-LO USAAF s/n 44-26969/N53753, which is seen in relatively intact condition on 13 November 1967 with its F-5G nose still in place. It had originally been built as a P-38L-5-LO before being sent to Dallas for conversion into the photo-recon role. The Lightning wound up in the huge Kingman, Arizona, scrapyard after the war, but survived to be sold surplus for $1500 in March 1946 to Aero Exploration Company of Tulsa, Oklahoma.

Soon after it went into service with Mark Hurd, a pioneer in aerial mapping. Hurd had also developed several types of cameras specifically for this mission and, as the USAAF had discovered, the P-38 was an excellent high-altitude photo platform. Hurd's P-38 fleet literally operated all over the globe on contracts that saw many areas being accurately mapped for the first time. N53753 is seen in the Hurd house colours of overall gray with blue trim.

Some sources claim that this aircraft was re-registered as N503MH in 1957, but it is obvious from this 1967 photo that the registration was not taken up. Hurd began to sell off its P-38 assets around the time this shot was taken, and N53753 went at a very low price to Bruce Pruett, a Lightning enthusiast from Livermore, California

RIGHT *The most picked-over Mark Hurd Lightning at Santa Barbara was N75551, which had been used as a spare parts 'Christmas tree' to keep the other Lightnings operational. This aircraft also started out life as P-38L-5-LO USAAF s/n 44-27083, before being converted into an F-5G-6-LO. It followed the same path as N53753 and wound up at Kingman, where it was purchased by Russell Reeves of Tulsa for $1500 on 8 April 1946. On 9 January 1947 the Lightning was bought by Mark Hurd and put to work in the photo-mapping role.*

N75551 completed many interesting mapping missions over the next 15 years, but by the time it was photographed in 1967 it was obviously in danger of extinction. Both props and the left Allison had been removed, along with the photo nose and numerous other parts. As can be seen, the Lightning had been fitted with a small raised canopy behind the pilot where the unfortunate equipment operator had to sit in what must have been an extremely uncomfortable space. The civilian Lightnings usually received individual modifications to suit particular contracts. N75551, along with N53753, was also purchased by Bruce Pruett in 1968 to become the basis for a very long restoration.

Pruett managed to accomplish some restoration work on his airframes, using N53753 as the main aircraft since it was the most complete. However, restoration of a Lightning is a daunting and money-absorbing project and in 1995 both Lightnings went to Jack Erickson's restoration facility in Medford, Oregon. In a deal worked out with Pruett, both aircraft will be restored – one flying example to be kept by Erickson for his collection, while the other will be returned to Pruett restored for static exhibition. Some sources state that this aircraft was re-registered as N502MH in 1957 but, as can be seen, the registration was never applied

BELOW RIGHT *Looking for all the world like it was ready to go on a mission when photographed at Santa Barbara on 12 July 1967, F-5G N517PA was finished in Hurd house colours, enlivened a bit by some high-viz DaGlo. By 1953, Mark Hurd had added a fifth Lightning to the company's fleet with the purchase of F-5G-6-LO USAAF s/n 44-53012 which, at the time, was registered N62441. This aircraft had also started out life as a P-38L before conversion at the Dallas modification centre. It is thought that the Lightning did not see much in the way of military service, and it was one of the first F-5s selected by a postwar operator,*

being purchased on 13 May 1946 from Kingman by Kargl Aerial Surveys of Midland, Texas.

By late 1947, ownership had transferred to Aero Exploration, who kept the fighter until it went to Mark Hurd. The crews that operated these Lightnings were a hardy bunch, often assigned to remote locations and flying the Lockheed twins to very high altitudes, where the two (and sometimes three) crewmembers would share extreme discomfort. Accordingly, it was decided to carry out an extremely extensive modification to N62441 and the aircraft was flown to AiResearch Aviation at Mines Field to have the fuselage pod heavily modified to incorporate pressurisation. The pilot's seat was moved forward and a second seat added behind so that the navigator could be accommodated in relative comfort. The canopy structure was heavily modified and enlarged, while the pressurisation system was run off a turbosupercharger. To accommodate the latter mod, the canopy was completely sealed and the crew had to enter through a small door cut in the fuselage. The system proved to work very well and allowed the crew to operate in much greater comfort.

Hurd changed the registration to N501MH during 1958 and flew the aircraft until 1965 when it went to Byers Airways, who quickly sold it on to Pacific Aerial Surveys of Seattle for $12,000. At this time, the registration was changed to N517PA, but the company went bankrupt in 1969. Obviously N517PA spent a good portion of its life after being sold by Hurd at Santa Barbara, so it is not certain just how much the F-5G was operated. In 1971 the Lightning went to Junior Burchinal of Paris, Texas, as a replacement for a P-38 he had written off during landing. In 1973 David Boyd of Tulsa, Oklahoma, was the registered owner, and by this time the aircraft was not in the best of condition, so it went to Starlite Aviation for a rebuild.

Boyd hoped to get the machine back into stock condition, but could not find an original fighter nose so a T-33 unit was adapted to fit – bringing the cockpit back to stock also proved to be too big a challenge. Painted in 459th FS colours, it was sold to Merrill Wien in 1981. By 1990 the P-38 had been sold to Yanks Air Museum at Chino, where it now occupies a portion of the organisation's display hangar. The museum's director, Stan Hoefler, plans to get the P-38 back into its original USAAF configuration as soon as 'I get about ten other airplanes restored!' In the meantime, the Lightning, now registered N718, is on display for all to see

ABOVE *Originally built as Lockheed P-38L-5-LO USAAF s/n 44-53078/N504MH is seen awaiting its next mission at Santa Barbara on 17 November 1962. Of interest are the two B-25 Mitchell fire-bombers on station in the background – this shot was taken prior to the type being banned in California following a series of structural failures.*

This aircraft is of particular interest since it was the first Lightning to be sold surplus following after World War 2 from the depot at Kingman. The buyer on 23 January 1946 was none other than famed test pilot (and pre-war race pilot) Tony LeVier, who registered the aircraft as NX21764 and flew it back to southern California so that it could be suitably modified for the Cleveland National Air Races. LeVier painted the aircraft bright red and stripped out as much unnecessary equipment as possible. Carrying race number 3, with the name FOX OF THE SKYWAYS, LeVier finished an impressive second in the Thompson Trophy Race for 1946 with a speed just a hair over 370 mph. In 1947 Tony won the Sohio Race and placed fifth in the Thompson. The races ended in 1949 with the disastrous crash of Bill Odum's highly-modified Mustang and the start of the Korean War in the following year.

Mark Hurd purchased the aircraft in 1953 and re-registered it as N504MH. After much hard work it was sold in 1965 (by which time it had gained a modified nose and a second miniature canopy behind the pilot for the navigator) to J Byron Roche. However, disaster was to strike on 4 August 1965 when horrified witnesses saw the Lightning plunge vertically out of a cloud deck with Roche trailing from his parachute, which had wrapped around the tail. The aircraft had been undergoing a test flight from Santa Barbara when, for unknown reasons, it crashed near Los Olivos. In a rather Phoenix-like ending, some mangled parts from this aircraft were salvaged in the early 1990s for inclusion in the restoration of Stephen Grey's Lightning, featured later in this volume

RIGHT *Photographed at Van Nuys Airport prior to the start of the 1947 Bendix Race, Tony LeVier's bright red Lightning NX21764 displays its nickname on the nose. The legend on the tail booms testifies to a second place win ('as good as first to us') in the 1946 Thompson Trophy Race*

BELOW RIGHT *Although it was never finished in the Mark Hurd scheme, N505MH was another of the company's fleet of hard-working Lightnings. Photographed on the ramp at Santa Barbara on 26 July 1962, the aircraft had been modified with a second seat behind the pilot, while retaining a basically stock F-5G nose. USAAF s/n 44-53186 was built as a P-38L-5-LO, before being transferred to Dallas for conversion into an F-5G-6-LO.*

This aircraft also wound up at Kingman following little USAAF use, and like a number of other Lightnings in this chapter, it followed a familiar road of ownership. It was purchased on 22 March 1946 by Kargl Aerial Surveys and registered N62350. By the end of 1947 the fighter was with Aero Exploration Company, who sold it on to Mark Hurd in 1952. In service with the latter it travelled the world on photo-mapping missions, and assumed the new identity of N505M during 1958.

In 1967 the aircraft was sold to Bill Harrah of Reno, Nevada, who owned a famous casino and had amassed a huge collection of vintage cars, displaying them in a world-class museum. Harrah also liked old aircraft and began adding a few to his collection. He purchased N505MH for $10,000 (which, at the time, was considered a high amount) and had famed airshow pilot Mira Slovak fly it to Reno.

After Harrah's death, the aircraft was sold in 1982 and went through several owners before being obtained by Doug Arnold's Warbirds of Great Britain. It was restored to flying condition at Chino and ferried across the Atlantic by Mike Wright in 1989. The P-38, now fitted with a fighter nose, was rarely displayed, and was soon sold to Evergreen Ventures of Marana, Arizona, during 1990.

Upon arrival (having once again been flown across the Atlantic by the stalwart Wright) in the US it was determined that the first restoration fell some way short of the company's exacting standards, so a decision was taken there and then to break the aircraft down to components and do a thorough ground-up rebuild. Now registered N38EV, the Lightning is still undergoing (as of this volume going to press) restoration at its Fort Collins, Colorado, home

ABOVE *Built as P-38L-5-LO USAAF s/n 44-53015, this aircraft was selected for conversion to F-5G-6-LO standards at Dallas. After accumulating very few flying hours, the Lightning was stored at Kingman for disposal. It was purchased in March 1946 by race car driver Rex Mays who had a desire to race the big Lightning. It was duly prepared for the 1946 Bendix Trophy Race and was entered as N57492 Race 55 with the name MacMillan Meteor. Flown by Mays, the red Lightning finished an unlucky 13th and its pilot apparently lost interest in air racing.*

During this immediate postwar period, quite a few civil-registered Lightnings simply 'disappeared', probably either being scrapped or sold overseas. In 1948 N57492 was deleted from the American civil register after it was supposedly exported to Costa Rica under the ownership of Robert Utterback. It is not known if the aircraft actually arrived in Costa Rica, or how what it was employed their. By 1954 it was back on the civil register as N9957F (note that N99**F series registrations were then applied to US civil aircraft operating overseas). The F-5G was then pur-

chased by Hycon Aerial Surveys of Pasadena, California, in 1955, who flew it for nearly ten years. The company operated several P-38s and the aircraft was modified with the hugely-extended nose seen in this photo. Hycon had numerous shadowy government contracts, and it is thought that some of the Lightning's overseas flights were done to obtain information for the fledgling Central Intelligence Agency. With the extended nose a variety of cameras and equipment could be carried, depending on the mission.

As the 1960s began, Hycon decided to get out of the P-38 business and the aircraft was flown to McCarran Field, Las Vegas, Nevada, for storage and possible sale. Las Vegas became home to several P-38s 'in transit', their respective owners probably being attracted by the low cost of tie-downs and the dry climate – the very distinctive N9957F was photographed here on 26 October 1963. Flags of various countries visited have been applied on the fuselage pod along with the addition of the word 'very' to the Limited license notice

ABOVE *During the early 1960s the most famous 'Hollywood fliers' of all time, Paul Mantz and Frank Tallman, decided to join forces and create Tallmantz Aviation at Orange County Airport is southern California. The two legendary pilots each brought with them large collections of vintage and veteran aircraft in various stages of airworthiness. Orange County, at that time, was a perfect location for the rag-tag air force of 'movie planes' since it was in a very rural setting and the field was also home to numerous similar aircraft. The partners thought Lockheed's twin-boom classic would be an ideal aircraft to join their flying collection and their newly-established 'Movieland of the Air'. A deal was struck to purchase the now rather-forlorn N9957F, and the aircraft was inspected for a ferry flight to Orange County in early 1964. It was sanded down and given a quick coat of silver paint, along with some inaccurate rudder stripes.*

While with Tallmantz the aircraft did not fly, and when the company ran into some financial difficulty, the P-38 was put up for auction along with numerous other aircraft. The Lightning then became the property of the Rosen Novak Auto Company, and an ad for the fighter attracted the attention of airline pilot Walter Erickson, who went to Orange County to inspect the aircraft. Despite its poor condition Erickson purchased the Lightning and, after some repairs, made a dangerous test

flight which saw one of the turbochargers catch fire. It was then ferried to Falcon Field in Mesa, Arizona – an ex-World War 2 Royal Air Force training base – where it was photographed during April 1968 amidst the many abandoned military aircraft that filled the site. At Falcon Erickson carried out further repairs, added drop tanks and flew the fighter to Minneapolis, where he removed the Hycon 'proboscis' and installed an F-5G nose in its place. In 1972 the P-38 was purchased by David Tallichet and flown to Chino where he replaced the F-5G nose with a fighter nose.

For the P-38's 40th anniversary in 1977 N9957F was flown very convincingly by Tony LeVier. As the value of the aircraft grew, Tallichet made a deal in 1980 in which he traded N9957F and P-47D N47TB to the USAF Museum in exchange for two C-130As. The aircraft was flown to McGuire AFB in New Jersey (being delayed after suffering a nose gear collapse along the way) where it was finished in the markings of second-ranking P-38 ace Maj Tom McGuire and, against the heavy protests of aviation enthusiasts worldwide, placed on a pole and left unprotected in the harsh New Jersey environment. Since then, despite repeated attempts to help 'preserve' the aircraft, the P-38's condition has steadily deteriorated due to general neglect, corrosion and repeated repairs by amateurs that have rendered the aircraft probably permanently non-airworthy

ABOVE *P-38L-5-LO USAAF s/n 44-53247 was selected for conversion to an F-5G-6-LO, and like most of the other photo-recon Lightnings in this book, flew only briefly before being assigned to the Kingman depot, where civilian buyers would try to find airframes with the least amount of flying hours on them – that is why the majority of colourfully-marked combat veterans did not survive. In February 1946 the F-5G was sold for $1500 to Wesley Grey of Long Beach, California. It was then resold to ex-WASP pilot Nancy Harkness-Love, but it is not known if the aircraft was flown during this short period.*

By the end of 1946 the fighter had once again changed hands to an ex-Grumman test pilot, who utilised the F-5G to test new avionics, radar units and camera installations. In 1951 the Lightning was sold once again, this time to Aero Service Corporation who operated a large fleet of surplus military aircraft on worldwide photo-mapping duties. The aircraft was flown for several years before being sold to the Virgil Kaufman Foundation in 1960. It was then traded to Bob Bean for a stock P-38M,

which was then presented to the USAF Museum. Bean flew his new prize to Blythe, California, where it was parked in one of the owner's desert storage bases, and it is thought never flown again.

Seen on 19 October 1967, the aircraft still retained its blue and yellow Aero Service markings and, except for its missing spinners and a few other panels, was essentially complete – the oxidized paint had by this stage become an ideal billboard for people who wanted to leave their name on the old fighter. In 1973 Bean traded the Lightning for six HU-16 Albatross amphibians, and the aircraft was trucked to Pima Air Museum in Tucson. Here, a volunteer force restored the aircraft to static display condition and finished it in a striking PRU Blue scheme.

Both the museum and its dedicated band of volunteers were dismayed when the USAF Museum took the P-38 back and sent it to the Musee de l'Air in Paris, France, where it was put in storage in mid-1989. Unfortunately, the storage hangar burned to the ground on 17 May 1990, destroying the Lightning, along with numerous other vintage aircraft

BELOW *Visitors to The Air Museum's site at Ontario Airport, California, in 1967 were treated to the rather amazing sight of a complete combat-ready P-38L, albeit a bit faded and corroded. USAAF s/n 44-26961 had been sold surplus in 1948 to the Fuerza Aerea Hondurena, along with several other P-38s.*

In 1960 Bob Bean, who has gone down in warbird legend as one of aviation's true eccentrics, struck a deal with Honduras that saw surplus Corsairs exchanged for the P-38s, plus several other vintage aircraft. While in Honduran service the P-38s were seldom flown, and were in stock condition when returned to the US. FAH 504 was transferred to The Air Museum, where it was displayed in full Honduran markings (the registration N74883 was assigned for the ferry flight but does not seem to have been placed on the aircraft), before being sold to Capt Laurence E Blumer of Washington in 1969.

Blumer was a wartime Lightning ace, having scored six kills with the 367th FG as part of the Ninth AAF in England in 1944. He had the aircraft finished as his old mount Scrap Iron IV, and the P-38 appeared at several airshows, including the 1971 Reno National Air Races.

Blumer soon sold the aircraft, however, and it went through several owners, gaining different registrations including N38DH and N6961, before winding up with warbird enthusiast John Deahl, who was killed when the Lightning crashed on 9 April 1981 after an engine failed on take-off. The wreckage was purchased by Kermit Weeks, who salvaged what he needed and then junked the res

RIGHT *The last Lightning operated by Mark Hurd Aerial Surveys was P-38L-5-LO USAAF s/n 44-53087, which was converted to P-38M-6-LO nightfighter status. However, despite the modification, this machine, along with a number of other M-models, was never employed nocturnally, their mission being undertaken by the Northrop P-61.*

Flown to Kingman for disposal, the fighter was one of 48 Lightnings purchased by Forrest Bird of Long Beach. Although Bird did operate at least one Lightning, and sold several others, it appears that the majority of the aircraft were purchased for their parts, and general scrap value – he had made a winning bid with the War Assets Administration and became the proud owner of 33 F-5Gs and 15 P-38Ms for approximately $1250 each.

Bird quickly sold off radios and other equipment, followed by the airframes themselves which went from $350 to $900 – he realised a good profit from his venture. Bird registered '087 as N62887 and sold the aircraft, which went through several other owners before winding up with Spartan Air Service in Canada. Spartan was another company that operated a variety of ex-military aircraft in the photo-mapping and survey roles, and they registered their P-38 as CF-GDS in June 1952. Spartan added their own photo nose and operated the fighter until 1956, when it was sold to Hycon Aerial Surveys as N1107V.

In 1958 N1107V became the property of Cartwright Aerial Surveys who fitted it with an expensive Zeiss mapping camera. Since this equipment was, at that time, worth more than the P-38, it was also fitted with its own parachute! In 1961 the aircraft went to Lefty Gardner and Lloyd Nolen to become the Confederate Air Force's first Lightning. In 1963 it was sold to Kucera & Associates of Cleveland, Ohio, who used the aircraft on mapping contracts in South America, and who extended the nose over 26 inches to accommodate another camera. In March 1967 the veteran was sold to A G Wilson and leased to Mark Hurd. This view shows the Spartan/Kucera photo nose to advantage

BELOW RIGHT *When photographed on 13 November 1967 at Santa Barbara, California, N1107V had been 'ridden hard and put away wet' as evidenced by the tremendous staining from the turbosuperchargers. After Hurd finished with the aircraft it went back to Wilson, who made a brief attempt to use the fighter as part of a warbird training school, before selling it to Peter Kahn.*

Kahn had been able to get an original fighter nose off a P-38 airframe that had been scrapped by MGM studios around 1970, and fitted the unit to N1107V, which was also re-registered as N3800L. In 1973 the P-38 went to warbird broker Jack Flaherty, who traded the craft to Wilson 'Connie' Edwards for a Hispano Ha-1112 Buchon – probably one of the worst warbird trades of recent times! In 1981 the Edwards family donated the P-38 to the EAA Museum in Oshkosh, Wisconsin, in memory of Bill Edwards, who was killed in the crash of a TF-51D Mustang

Lightning with Nine Lives

ABOVE *Over the years, Burbank Airport, home to the majority of P-38s built, has occasionally been host to a surviving Lightning or two such as N5596V, seen undergoing a ground run on its left Allison V-1710 during April 1969. This particular aircraft had been built at Burbank as P-38L-5-LO USAAF s/n 44-26996, and was accepted by the military during April 1945 and then assigned to the Dallas modification depot where it was converted to an F-5G-6-LO. As with other aircraft in this book, the near new Lightning was ferried to Kingman for disposal at the end of the war.*

Thousands of ex-military aircraft were located at Kingman, the majority of which were simply scrapped on site with absolutely no thought given to preserving some of the colourful combat veterans for the enjoyment and study of future generations. Aero Explorations of Tulsa inspected the near-new '996 and purchased it, registering the aircraft as N53752. Aero were the first operators of the F-5G, but like many other surviving P-38s, it soon began to shuttle between new owners, first going to Canada's Spartan Air Service as CF-GCH in 1952, where it was

operated as a high-altitude mapping aircraft until 1956 when the company decided to standardize on surplus RCAF de Havilland Mosquitos.

The fighter then went to Hycon Aerial Surveys as N5596V for continued aerial work, but in 1959 N5596V, along with its stablemates, were put out to pasture and flown to Las Vegas, Nevada, for storage and sale. Over the next few years the aircraft passed through many hands until it found a 'new' home with Junior Burchinal in Paris, Texas, on 19 August 1970.

The colourful Burchinal, a preacher who operated the local truck stop, also ran the Flying Tigers Air Museum, which offered instruction in a variety of ex-wartime aircraft, so the Lightning was an ideal choice. However, the strip at Paris was of the grass and dirt variety, and being only 3000 ft long some of the students literally got the rides of their life as they were checked out in aircraft as diverse as a Corsair, Mustang and Bearcat.

During May 1971 Burchinal had the P-38 up for a quick flight and, knowing that his strip was wet with rain from a thunderstorm, decided to shut down both engines on landing and let the aircraft roll to a stop. However, a car pulled out in front of the P-38 and Burchinal managed to get one engine going and put the aircraft in a skid, missing the vehicle but coming to rest on US Highway 82, minus the landing gear. Since traffic was blocked, the P-38 was hurriedly pulled off the tarmac with a tractor, which inflicted considerable damage. It was then rather unceremoniously dumped in the weeds at the edge of the field

Over the years N5596V became a sad sight at the airfield, and parts were sold off the airframe to aid in another restoration, but in 1979 the wreck was purchased by John Silberman with the goal of getting it flying. He faced a daunting task as many parts were gone, including everything forward of the firewalls. The hydraulic system was also missing, the cockpit gutted, the landing gear torn out and numerous small parts long since sold. Finally, the hulk had suffered skin damage both during and since the accident. Silberman and Thurston 'Jaybo' Hinyub put in thousands of hours searching for parts and rebuilding what they had. Finally, a reborn N5596V attended the 1986 Valiant Air Command get together in Titusville, Florida – it is seen here fight during the show with Don Davidson's P-51D-20-NA N51EA Double Trouble Two

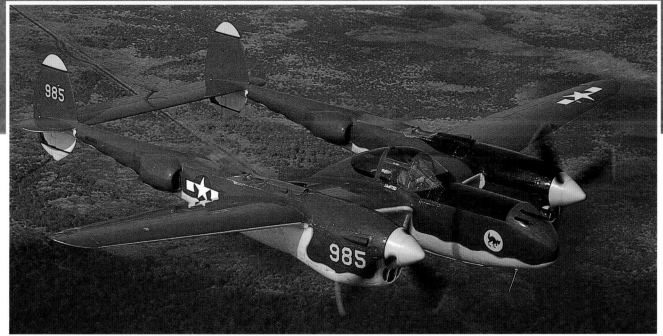

ABOVE *A deal was struck between Silberman and the Museum of Flying in Santa Monica that saw N5596V sold on 11 October 1989. Now, just one problem remained – getting the P-38 from Florida to California. Alan Preston and Bruce Lockwood went to Florida to prepare the aircraft, and found the fighter needed lots of work.*

'Bruce tore into the innards of the thing', said Preston when interviewed for this book, 'and we kept finding more and more items that had to be repaired. When we were finally ready for the ferry flight, it was something of a thrill. I had never flown a P-38, but had spent a lot of time looking over the manuals and talking to Tony LeVier. Still, the aircraft was a handful. I had seven engine failures heading west and began to think I was going to log more single-engine time in the plane than twin-engine time. Still, with Bruce following, we eventually made it to Clover Field, got the plane in a hangar, and really began tearing it apart'

RIGHT *'Once we began tearing into the airframe and engines', said Preston, 'we decided to repair or replace many items. One of our first decisions was to get rid of that awful nose and the green paint scheme. However, finding a fighter nose was impossible so, fortunately with the help of Steve Hinton, we were able to borrow The Air Museum's fighter nose and build our own.*

The metal work was done by Phil Greenburg'. As can be seen, the nose did not turn out like the original in contour or in panel detail. Alan Preston is pictured flying N5596V back from Santa Maria, where the P-38 had been flown to receive its new paint scheme

ABOVE *N5596V displays its classic lines on the ramp, this high-angle view showing the deletion of the turbosuperchargers to advantage, along with the design's generous flap area. For the auction, the P-38 was finished in a 435th FS paint scheme. The machine helped generate a great deal of publicity for the 1990 Museum of Flying Auction, which drew bidders from around the world to view a very wide variety of classic aircraft that were being put under the hammer.*

When the P-38 was rolled into the auction tent a great deal of excitement was generated as the fighter was introduced by several aces who had flown the type. Bidding started quickly and proceeded briskly, with Gen William Lyons taking the winning bid at $1,550,000 – one of the highest prices ever paid for a warbird, and showing how the trend had reversed from Mustangs being at the top end of the price scale. Lyons had his prize flown to John Wayne Airport (formerly Orange County Airport) where it was put on display. Seldom flown, the aircraft was made ready for a flight to a P-38 pilots' reunion in 1992, but the fighter suffered a belly landing at Winslow, Arizona, after pilot John Crocker could not get the landing gear lowered. Fortunately the aircraft was repaired and is, as of this writing, still on display at John Wayne

RIGHT *Escorts from Santa Maria to Santa Monica join up with the P-38, including Chuck Smith in the T-28 Trojan and Bruce Lockwood in the P-51D Mustang. Several television crews were on hand at Clover Field for the arrival of the P-38, which was to be one of the main attractions in the 1990 Museum of Flying vintage and veteran aircraft auction*

PUTT-PUTT MARU

RIGHT *A visitor to remote Blythe Airport in the California desert near the Arizona border on 27 October 1967 would have seen P-38M-6-LO USAAF s/n 44-53095 in full, but faded, markings of the air force of Honduras. It originally started out life as a P-38L and was apparently selected for conversion to two-seat P-38M nightfighter status. However, an examination of the airframe did not show any of the modifications, and one wonders if this aircraft was ever so converted because it would have been unusual postwar to revert it back to stock P-38L status.*

After the end of the war there was a brief flurry of profitable business to be had in supplying ex-US military aircraft to Latin America. Some of these transactions were undertaken by the government, and some by private individuals. The air force of Honduras was, before the war, operating a

rag-tag collection of aircraft including a few dating from World War 1! However, because of its strategic location, the US supplied a variety of new training aircraft during the war. After 1945, Honduras wanted fighter equipment, especially in light of its strained relations with neighbouring countries. Eventually, at least six P-38s and three P-63s were transferred to Honduras. These were part of a package sold by Col Malcolm Stewart, a former commander of the Fuerza Aerea Hondurena, and the P-38s came from a group of machines located in Miami. Some sources indicate that '095 received the registration N67745, but details from this time period are either lost or forgotten.

The P-38s were rarely flown in FAH service, and dealing began with Bob Bean to supply F4U-4 Corsairs in their place since it was thought that these radial-engine warriors would be easier to operate in the hot and humid climate than the Allison V-12s. It wasn't until 1959 that a deal was finally struck, however, and five P-38s, two P-63s and a Lockheed Model 10A were transferred to Bean's ownership and flown to the US. The P-38s joined Bean's warbird collection at Blythe, and '095 was registered N9005R and parked in the harsh desert climate

LEFT A man of unorthodox religious views, Bean was in no hurry to part with his prizes, but after years of badgering collector Bill Ross eventually acquired N9005R in 1969. The P-38 headed to Chicago where Ross was based. Logs indicated that it had flown less than 100 hours, so the airframe was in good condition. Ross had his crew go through it before debuting the fighter in 1972. By 1986 he had sold it to the Lone Star Flight Museum in Texas. Museum director Jim Fausz stated, 'The P-38 was in less than ideal condition when it arrived, and it was decided to tear down the airframe and go through all systems'. The aircraft finally emerged from the restoration shop as 475th FG 27-kill Pacific ace Col Charles MacDonald's PUTT PUTT MARU

ABOVE *On one of its first airshow outings, Ronnie Gardner banks* PUTT PUTT MARU *around a cloud near Breckenridge, Texas, on 25 May 1991. MacDonald's aircraft was extremely colourful, and that's one of the reasons why the museum chose his markings – the other was to honour America's seventh-ranking World War 2 ace.*

RIGHT *For all its size and weight, the P-38 is quite manoeuvrable, and its twin Allisons were a definite advantage during the war in the Pacific, where long over-water flights were a daily occurrence. Also, the heavy armament was particularly effective against lightly-armoured Japanese aircraft and shipping. Lone Star maintains its aircraft to a very high standard, and all their warbirds are attractively displayed in two huge climate-controlled hangars in Galveston*

BELOW RIGHT *Of the few Lightnings still flying,* PUTT PUTT MARU *is one of the finest. Current Lone Star director Ralph Royce states that, 'the P-38 is one of our most popular aircraft and is frequently requested for airshows around the country. However, because of its rarity and high operating cost, we are very careful about building up flying hours on the airframe'*

Night Lightning

ABOVE *As mentioned in the previous chapter, it appears that PUTT PUTT MARU may never have been converted into a two-seat P-38M nightfighter, but there is no doubt that USAAF s/n 44-53097 was converted into a radar-equipped nocturnal hunter. The aircraft started out as P-38L-5-LO, before being assigned for conversion to P-38M, status but few hours were put on the airframe before it was assigned to Kingman. Aircraft '097 was one of a batch of 11 Lightnings purchased by Dick Martin and R A Wardell for possible resale. Five machines were purchased by an outfit in Miami, and Dick and other pilots ferried the aircraft to Florida, including '097.*

The P-38M was registered N67861 for the ferry flight to Miami, where it was prepared for military service with Honduras. It was eventually coded FAH 503, but as with rest of the FAH P-38 and P-63 fleet, was seldom, if ever, flown. As with the remaining FAH P-38s, FAH 503 was acquired by Bob Bean and flown to his Blythe facility, where it is seen on 29 October 1967 with the second seat for the radar operator clearly visible

BOTTOM *As with the rest of the Bean P-38s, FAH 503, which had been registered N9011R, was simply parked on his ramp and left, although the eccentric Bean would occasionally perform some work on the airframes. In FAH service the P-38M was not operated as a nightfighter, and it appears that the radar equipment had been removed before delivery to that country. The FAH had a difficult time operating even day fighters, so the operation of one nightfighter was out of the question. With its tail nearly touching the desert sand, the P-38M is seen on 27 December 1962 at Blythe. Note*

how both canopies have become yellowed due to exposure to the sun. The P-38M carried an interesting nose insignia consisting of a large bird with a gun and telescope

BELOW *By 27 October 1967 the P-38M had begun to shed parts, and it is seen on the Blythe ramp in company with a few of Bean's other warbirds, including the ex-Aero Services F-5G N90813 and an F4U-4 Corsair*

RIGHT *Dick Martin became acquainted with the P-38M once again after Bean sold the aircraft in 1968. It went through a couple of owners without ever leaving Blythe. However, Thomas Freidkin purchased N9011R in 1971, and contracted with Martin to have it restored back to flying condition at Van Nuys, California. Martin and his crew did an excellent job and the fighter made its first post-restoration flight during September 1972. N9011R is seen at Freidkin's Palomar, California, home base during August 1973. At the time it was unpainted, and the second seat canopy had been replaced with a new unit moulded in a particularly hideous shade of green*

LEFT *Freidkin had N9011R re-registered N7TF, and the M-model was painted in a truly awful new scheme as shown in this November 1973 photo taken at Palomar. Even though N7TF was an extremely rare machine, Freidkin decided to part ownership with it, selling the P-38M to John Boulton of Orlando, Florida, in 1974, who once again re-registered it, this time as N3JB*

LEFT *Boulton in turn sold the P-38M to collector John Stokes of San Marcos, Texas, in 1974, and the aircraft acquired its new silver and red paint scheme, along with this attractive* Der Gabelshwanz Teufel *(fork tailed devil) insignia. During these various transactions, the P-38M was not flown much, but it did make an appearance in the television series* Black Sheep Squadron *in the late 1970s, where it was flown by Dick Martin, Tom Freidkin and Steve Hinton. Stokes soon put the fighter up for sale, advertising it as 'the only one in the world' that could be yours for $250,000 – most collectors at the time regarded this price as overly high. The aircraft was sold in 1978 to Cecil Harp and Robert Ennis, but was again put on the market after Ennis was killed in a Catalina crash*

ABOVE *Fortunately, the next owner for the P-38M was Doug Champlin's Fighter Museum in Mesa, Arizona, which is home to a fabulous collection of aircraft kept in flying condition, but not flown. The museum purchased the fighter in 1983, and as this book went to press, the management of the collection has been taken over by a new company, and it was uncertain if the museum would stay at Mesa or, for that matter, even in the United States. Museum director Jim Fausz was instrumental in obtaining the P-38M for the museum, and he is seen in the cockpit during February 1984 prior to one of its very few flights under museum ownership*

Jim Fausz airborne in the P-38M over Mesa during February 1984. Doug Champlin felt that the M-model did not fit into the museum's fighter aces theme so, in 1987, the decision was made to convert the Lockheed back to P-38L status, and Champlin was able to trade parts with John Stokes, who was helping bring a derelict P-38J back to life in Texas – the M's second seat and bubble were incorporated into the rebuild of the J, and the Fighter

Museum wound up with a beautiful P-38L that is now accurately finished

in the markings of 475th FG seven-kill ace John 'Jack' Purdy, and is on

display for all admirers of what is perhaps Lockheed's most famous design

Saga of
JOLTIN' JOSIE

ABOVE RIGHT *As stated earlier in this volume, there were certain colourful and eccentric individuals who, after the end of World War 2, purchased ex-military aircraft, and thus ensured the survival of some of these classic machines. One such character was Jack Hardwick who ran an aviation parts business in El Monte, California. Referring to himself as 'The Mad Man Muntz of the Air' (for those thus uninitiated, 'Mad Man Muntz' was a postwar Los Angeles wheeler-dealer who ran a series of discount stores specialising in sales of newly-emerging televisions, and who even designed and produced his own automobile, known as the 'Muntz Jet'), a term he painted on at least one of his racing aircraft.*

Hardwick purchased surplus fighters and bombers and entered several in the Cleveland Air Races, where he enjoyed varying degrees of success, walking away from one violent crash landing. Hardwick purchased P-38J-20-LO USAAF s/n 44-23314 from the Hancock College of Aeronautics in Santa Maria, California. The airfield had been a wartime P-38 training base, and the school had a large collection of ex-wartime warriors on which their students could work. Hardwick got the aircraft in April 1954 and registered it NL29Q. The Lightning was made marginally airworthy and flown to Brackett Field, California, where it was parked in the weeds next to Lightning N79123. Neither aircraft was going anywhere, so Hardwick donated NL29Q to Ed Maloney's The Air Museum in 1959.

The aircraft was complete, but in need of lots of care, which Maloney did not have the money or facilities for at the time. The P-38 was moved to several locations as Maloney sought a permanent home, which finally became Chino Airport, and NL29Q is seen in less than perfect condition at that location during July 1974. As the fighter was being towed to its new residence from nearby Ontario Airport, the left main gear leg collapsed, resulting in a bent prop blade and damage to the nacelle and landing gear doors

BELOW RIGHT *N29Q starting to look like a real Lightning once again in the Fighter Rebuilders hangar. The shop space had to be extended so th t the big Lightning could be accommodated. Here, a freshly-overhauled JRS Allison V-1710 awaits i stallation*

ABOVE *Lockheed designers did an excellent job cowling (and cooling) the Allison V-1710 V-12 powerplants. Both propellers revolved towards the fuselage pod, thus eliminating the chronic torque swing problems (particularly on take-off) experienced by pilots flying most single-engine wartime fighters. Of course, if an engine quit at an inappropriate moment, the pilot of a combat-loaded P-38 would find his hands quite full*

Restoring a P-38 back to flying condition is an extremely expensive proposition because the Lightning is a complex machine and has virtually two of everything to rebuild! In 1986, a campaign was started to get the tired fighter back into the air, and businessman, and ex-wartime US Navy pilot, Bob Pond, stepped forward to generously supply the majority of funds needed to complete the project.

The aircraft was moved into Steve Hinton's Fighter Rebuilders shop (adjacent to the museum) and work began at a feverish pace, resulting in a first post-restoration flight on 22 July 1988. Steve Hinton likes nothing better than flying tight formation, evident in this view of the aircraft's third test flight as Steve brings the P-38 in for a close inspection of the photographer sat in the tail of a Mitchell

ABOVE *While the P-38 was being prepared for our July 1988 photo flight, work continued on other museum aircraft, including replacing a tyre that had gone flat on the Lightning and getting the Mustang ready for a test hop*

RIGHT *The slim, streamlined, fuselage pod of the Lightning not only housed the pilot but also the weapons, ammunition and radios. To ease cockpit access for a combat pilot weighed down with his parachute, 'Mae West' and survival harness, both canopy side panels opened out and the roof panel hinged back. The retractable step used to enter and exit the cockpit is seen stowed at the extreme top rear portion of the pod*

Over a southern California fog bank, Steve Hinton departs Chino in JOLTIN' JOSIE *during November 1988. The installation of the piping and turbosuperchargers is evident in this view, as well as the overall sleekness of the design. NX38BP divides its time between Chino, Palm Springs and Pond's Planes of Fame East in Minnesota*

RIGHT *Here's what greeted visitors to Fighter Rebuilders during July 1987 – a rusted, corroded, pile of bits and pieces that had once been Lockheed F-5C-1-LO USAAF s/n 42-67543. The aircraft was delivered to the USAAF as a P-38J at Burbank during October 1943 and then assigned to the Lockheed facility at Love Field, Dallas, for conversion to an F-5C. It appears that after conversion, the aircraft never left the US, going from the 36th PRS at Muskogee, Oklahoma, to the 379th Base Unit at Coffeyville, Kansas, and then into some form of storage.*

It was apparently sold to an unknown buyer and then probably flown on a ferry flight to Austin, Texas, where it began to sink into the ground. The aircraft was abandoned at Ragsdale Flying Service in Austin, and gradually vandalised and picked to pieces. In the mid-1960s, the airframe was acquired by Lefty Gardner and transferred to Mercedes, Texas, where it remained in the open for many years.

In 1988 what was left of the aircraft was sold to noted British collector Stephen Grey for his Duxford-based The Fighter Collection. Grey had contracted Fighter Rebuilders to work on other aircraft in the past, so a deal was struck that saw the airframe move to Chino

Lightning
Over Duxford

LEFT *Steve Hinton and his crew at Fighter Rebuilders had not realised how lucky they had been with the rebuild of Lightning NL29Q, featured in the previous chapter – at least they had started with an aircraft that was basically complete and structurally sound. While the finishing touches were being applied to that Lightning, a pile of parts arrived in a truck at Hinton's Chino hangar, and some observers were surprised when those parts were proclaimed to be a P-38. Fewer even believed that the pile would grow into a magnificent flying aircraft – but they were wrong as John Dibbs' photograph of P-38J-10-LO USAAF s/n 42-67543 over a Duxford, England, cloud bank proves* (John Dibbs)

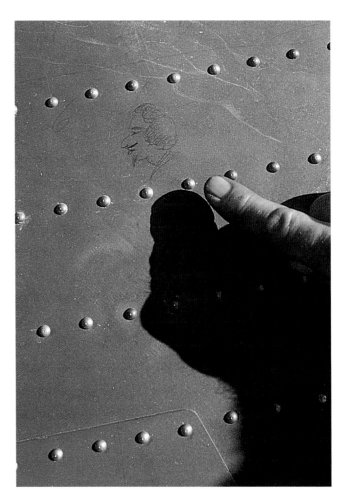

LEFT *Once at Chino the airframe was carefully broken down into components. Some interior parts were in surprisingly good condition, thanks to a protective coat of zinc chromate applied at the factory 40 years before. During the war it was not uncommon for 'Rosie the Riveter' to add pencilled notes, drawings or phone numbers that would, hopefully, be read by pilots and crews. This doodle of a cartoon character was found on an inside panel of the centre section, and is pointed out by a Chino worker*

RIGHT *Photo of the right vertical shows the ravages of time, including some bullet holes picked up whilst the airframe served as a makeshift target in Texas. 'P26' was a factory code applied at Dallas, while the legend SOUTH PACIFIC was painted on sometime later. Europe was painted on the left boom, indicating that the F-5C could have been displayed as a memorial at some point in its obscure past*

BELOW *The completely stripped-down centre section of the F-5C is seen at Chino during March 1988. Steve and his crew made a careful inventory of all missing parts and components that needed replacing or rebuilding. A visitor to Fighter Rebuilders during this time period would be greeted by the rather remarkable sight of two P-38s being restored to flying condition*

THESE PAGES AND PREVIOUS SPREAD *Once fully restored and thoroughly air-tested, the Lightning was crated up and sent across the Atlantic by ship to England in March 1992. Once Stephen Grey had become familiar with his new fighter, he initially had it marked up in the bare metal scheme of eight-kill 1st FG ace, Jack Ilfrey.*

For the 1994 season, Grey decided to refinish the Lightning in an Olive Drab and Neutral Grey camouflage scheme which would protect the airframe in the damp English weather – the spectacular result was California Cutie. *The polished nose cone was applied by pilots hoping to fool Luftwaffe fighters into thinking that their aircraft were unarmed photo-recon Lightnings. The original* California Cutie *of 1944 was flown by Lt Richard Loehnert of the 55th FS/20th FG, Eighth AAF, whilst the modern day version is put through its paces in this sequence by Hoof Proudfoot and Carl Schofield* (Photos by John Dibbs)

ABOVE *For Cleveland the aircraft had its camera nose replaced with a gun nose, but according to Walling, flew eight mph slower! However, more modifications were to come and these included clipping the wings and tail, moving the carburettor air scoops, adding new exhaust stacks, water injection, and numerous other modifications to create* Sky Ranger, *probably the most attractive off all P-38 racers. During qualifications, Walling hit 440 mph, but in the process burned off the majority of the exhaust stacks, so new units were added that were not as sophisticated and caused considerable drag. Walling dropped out of the Thompson Trophy Race on the second lap due to numerous problems, but with further modifications, the F-5G competed in the 1948 and 1949 races. With the cancellation of the Cleveland event, many racing P-38s simply disappeared*

OVERLEAF *Reed sold N25Y to Hugh Wells of Baltimore, Maryland, in 1953, and the aircraft remained at that location for nine years, seldom, if ever, flying while the ownership changed several times. With drop tanks installed, and some of its racing modifications still in place, N25Y is seen at Baltimore during March 1959*

Lefty's Lightning

BELOW White Lightnin' is seen over Madera, California, during August 1986 with its smoke system on. Delivered as F-5G-6-LO USAAF s/n 44-53254, the aircraft only served with the USAAF from July to September 1945 before being ferried to Kingman for disposal. Purchased in April 1946 for $1250 by Lilee Products of Chicago for unknown purposes, the aircraft received the civil registration of N25Y, but was sold in just a few months to J D Reed for the odd price of $1565.85 – the new owner had purchased several other ex-fighters and wanted to go racing at Cleveland.

Reed had a Beechcraft dealership in Houston and was also involved in other Texas business activities, and he hired Charlie Walling to fly N25Y in the January 1947 Miami All-American Air Manoeuvres. Beside a spectacular paint scheme, the aircraft was basically stock, but it nevertheless came in second. Reed decided to heavily modify the aircraft for the 1947 Cleveland event

ABOVE *In 1962 Vernon Thorpe purchased the fighter and flew it for about a year before selling the aircraft to Marvin 'Lefty' Gardner and two partners for the sum of $4000. 'Lefty' flew a variety of combat aircraft during World War 2 and after returning to civilian life opened a Texas ag business that is still going strong today.*

Gardner was a founding member of the Confederate Air Force (CAF), and N25Y was finished in the their 'official' colours of red, white, and blue – a scheme it still carries today, although with some revisions. In

1971 'Lefty' and N25Y became a regular at the Reno National Air Races, both as competitors and airshow performers. 'Lefty' announced his retirement from Reno in 1994, but after a rethink in early 1995, decided to 'unretire' himself for that year's event. He is seen flying N25Y near Harlingen, Texas, during October 1975

RIGHT *The Lightning is kept company by two Hawker Sea Furys near Harlingen during October 1976*

ABOVE 'Lefty' and N25Y participated in the second annual Phoenix 500 air race, where he qualified the P-38 at a very respectable 372.535 mph, and went on to place second in the stock race on 26 March 1995 at 318.142 mph.

The aircraft is seen on the ramp at Phoenix Goodyear Airport, Arizona, on 17 March 1995, during the lead up to race week. This historic field used to be NAS Litchfield Park, where the majority of the US Navy's burgeoning wartime air fleet was stored, and later scrapped

LEFT N25Y is the only P-38 currently flying with the low profile chin cowlings carried by early variants of the Lightning

RIGHT Lefty sits on the right wing of his trusty Lightning while being towed into the pits following the completion of the stock race at the 1995 Phoenix 500 event

Those Rare 'Razorbacks'

BELOW *Seen in rather 'plain Jane' markings during November 1965 at Ontario, California, The Air Museum's Curtiss-built Republic P-47G (USAAF s/n 42-25234) Thunderbolt originally saw Stateside service with training units – it appears that the majority of Curtiss-built Thunderbolts were similarly employed – before being sent to Grand Central Air Terminal, which was Los Angeles' main airline airport before improvements to Mines Field resulted in Los Angeles Airport, now LAX. As an aside, Glendale's wonderful Art Deco tower still stands intact, but abandoned, waiting for an owner who will hopefully preserve the structure.*

Whilst here '234 was utilised, along with a number of other former military aircraft, as a mechanics' training aid by Cal-Aero Technical Institute. The aircraft had not flown all that much in military service, and at the school it was used to teach engine start procedures, as well as for the study of hydraulics and electrical systems. By 1955 the aircraft had started to deteriorate, and the writing was on the wall for the airport – civilisation had completely encroached around the field, and complaints about noise and accidents were numerous. During this time period Glendale was home to literally hundreds of military aircraft as several companies overhauled machines as diverse as Mustangs and C-46 Commandos for the US military, as well as foreign air forces

ABOVE *With John Maloney at the controls, NX3395G forms tightly on the Bonanza camera-ship while Steve Hinton flies wing in Bob Pond's immaculate Thunderbolt during July 1986.*

John's father, Ed Maloney, had started gathering historic aircraft and artifacts after the end of World War 2 when such items had little monetary or sentimental value, and were often simply junked. Naturally, Maloney was attracted to the now rare aircraft held by Cal-Aero, including the Thunderbolt, and a deal was struck in 1955 that saw the P-47G transferred to the fledgling The Air Museum at Claremont, California.

The aircraft was not flyable at this point, but it was restored to airworthy condition by 1963, although flights were fairly infrequent. At that time, this was the only flying Thunderbolt except for P-47D USAAF s/n 42-23278/N5087V, which was part of the vast fleet of warbirds owned by Bob Bean. It was made airworthy for manufacturer's Republic Aviation, who flew it a few times, and even had the fighter shipped to the Paris Airshow, where it was exhibited in 1963. The aircraft's registration was changed to N347D in the early 1960s, before being finally grounded and donated by Republic to the USAF Museum in 1964, where it remains to this day

ABOVE *When doing air-to-air missions with Chino-based aircraft, one of the most common 'join up' points is nearby Lake Matthews, an easily recognisable geographical feature that readily stands out in the smog that plagues the San Gabriel Valley. In this May 1985 view Don Lykins is flying the aircraft, which is finished in the markings of World War 2 (21 kills) and Korean War (3.5 kills) ace Walker 'Bud' Mahurin. 'Bud' has been a long-time supporter of The Air Museum, and it is appropriate that the 'T-Bolt' carries his 'UN-M' codes (63rd FS/56th FG) and the name* SPIRIT OF ATLANTIC CITY, NJ.

Don Lykins was more recently the test pilot for The Air Museum's magnificent Northrop N9M Flying Wing restoration. During 1995 The Air Museum opened an auxiliary museum at the Grand Canyon in Arizona. Located at Valle Airport, the new facility boasts an interesting selection of aircraft, one of which is the P-47G

ABOVE RIGHT *As the warbird movement slowly began to grow during the early 1970s, The Air Museum was often called upon to display its historic aircraft at various military open houses. NX3395G is seen being fuelled at NAS Miramar, California, on 15 March 1971. Note the large access panel that has been removed on the side of the fuselage. During its lengthy ownership by The Air Museum, the Thunderbolt has gone through several sets of markings – the codes worn here are for an 82nd FS/78th FG machine*

RIGHT *Remote General William Fox Field in Lancaster, California, is often used for warbird training, and NX3395G is seen at the field on 17 October 1971 in revised markings with the name* ROSCOE'S RETREAT. *The term 'razorback' came from the rather sharp definition of the upper fuselage decking as it met with the built-up canopy*

Just under a week after the NX3395G was seen in Lancaster it attended the popular annual airshow at NAS Point Mugu in southern California. Whilst performing his display Roscoe Diehl experienced total power loss when the R-2800 suffered a massive engine failure – he quickly found out why wartime aviators often called the P-47 'the flying brick'.

Roscoe, a skilled professional pilot, had few choices and little time in which to act since he was already at a low altitude when the engine failed. Knowing he could not make the safety of Mugu's huge concrete runways, Roscoe headed for a small, ploughed farm field bordering a highway. With gear and flaps down, he had his hands full keeping the Thunderbolt upright as it skipped and jumped over the dirt furrows. Unfortunately, a vertical concrete water pipe was in the way and the stricken fighter impacted with the immovable object before coming to rest against the road's embankment.

Although appearing fairly intact in these photographs, the P-47 received major structural damage and was stored for several years before funding could be raised to begin the rebuild process

ABOVE *This detail view of the P-47G's V-shaped windshield shows that Mahurin's wartime markings have been faithfully reproduced on The Air Museum's 'T-Bolt'*

OPPOSITE *Few who saw the hulk of this 'razorback' P-47 at Palomar Airport during July 1976 ever thought that the gutted remains would once again take to the air. After the war, many Latin American countries began to scramble for more modern military equipment, some taking advantage of favoured nation status and obtaining aircraft directly from the US government, while others took more shadowy paths.*

In 1949 tattered 'razorback' TP-47D-2-RE, USAAF s/n 42-8205, was purchased from a storage lot at Clinton, Oklahoma, by the Texas Railroad and Equipment Company. The fighter was restored to airworthy condition, given the civilian registration NC75640, and flown to Bolling

AFB in Washington DC. At this time some sort of deal was struck with the Bolivian government and the P-47D was purchased for the Fuerza Aerea Boliviana, but the next problem was how to get it from Washington DC to Bolivia. An ex-USAAF pilot was hired for the task and the 'T-Bolt' eventually made it to La Paz, where it joined a few AT-6s and Curtiss SNC-1s, as well as examples of 1930s' CW-14 Ospreys, Falcons, and Hawk IIs.

The political situation in Bolivia at that time did not lend itself to obtaining ex-warplanes directly from the US government, so attempts were made to get P-47s and P-51s through 'brokers' in America. A deal to get more 'T-Bolts' fell through and the 'razorback' remained the sole example of its type in Bolivia. It did not fly again, instead being used as training aid, before being put on display as a gate-guard at El Alto, where it acquired a shark's mouth and James Bond 007 coding!

BELOW *As the warbird movement grew in the United States, several collectors attempted to purchase the gate-guard 'razorback', but these fell through, although a deal was finally struck with Jim Cullen in 1973 and the aircraft was disassembled and shipped to the US.*

In 1976 the remains of the aircraft were obtained by Doug Champlin to join his growing collection of vintage and veteran aircraft. It was shipped to Palomar, California, where rebuilding took place, and the Thunderbolt is seen on the ramp in July 1980 in basically complete condition – note the missing belly skin which covered the turbosupercharger. The aircraft made its first flight in 1981

RIGHT *Doug Champlin had the Thunderbolt registered N14519 and ferried to his new Champlin Fighter Museum at Mesa, where it was painted in the attractive, and accurate, wartime markings of Lt Col Robert Baseler's* BIG STUD *– he was the commanding officer of the 325th FG.*

The museum's aircraft are all maintained in airworthy condition, but seldom flown. Fortunately, the completed machine was flown briefly in October 1981 so that Jim Larsen could take aerial photographs of this magnificently restored survivor (Jim Larsen)

LEFT Set against a magnificent cloud backdrop and accompanied by Pete Regina's P-51B Mustang, Ray Stutsman displays the classic lines of TP-47G USAAF s/n 42-25068 N47DG over California's Central Valley during August 1983.

Like Ed Maloney's aircraft, this Curtiss-built Thunderbolt was given to the Oakland Technical School in Oakland, California, during 1946 for use as a mechanics' training aid. However, by 1952 the airframe had been obtained by Jack Hardwick, an ex-wartime aircraft parts dealer, who moved it to his storage yard in El Monte, California, following a brief spell as an engine test stand for the new Flying Tiger Line at Burbank Airport.

The aircraft remained at this location until 1975 when it was obtained by Eagle Aviation of Tulsa, Oklahoma, where some initial restoration work was begun

INSET In 1979 '068 was purchased by Ray Stutsman of Elkhart, Indiana, for a ground-up restoration. While taking the Thunderbolt apart at his Indiana restoration shop, Stutsman found a bag of cardboard gun barrel plugs left behind by workers at the Curtiss factory!

The restored fighter made its first post-rebuild flight during April 1982, and was finished in the Olive Drab and Neutral Grey camouflage of an aircraft flown by 18-kill ace Capt W C Beckham of the 351st FS/353rd FG, who named his mount LITTLE DEMON.

In 1987 Stutsman sold his Thunderbolt to the Lone Star Flight Museum, and the aircraft is currently maintained in airworthy condition at the museum's impressive Galveston headquarters

Yugoslavian Veteran

BELOW *Nearing the end of a ground-up restoration, P-47D USAAF s/n 42-26766 is seen on 5 September 1992 outside Bill 'Tiger' Destefani's restoration facility at Minter Field, Shafter, California. The ex-wartime training base is home to a number of warbirds and unlimited racing aircraft, while an annual warbird show is held every April that attracts a wide variety of vintage aircraft. This particular machine was obtained in very poor condition from Yugoslavia where it had been on display in a park. Instead of using spray paint cans to apply graffiti, the Yugoslavians apparently prefer chisels, and names and slogans where chiselled over the entire airframe, which meant that a great deal of skin had to be replaced*

RIGHT *Detail view of the engine mount, firewall and some of the installed engine accessories on the aircraft. On 14 November 1951 Yugoslavia signed a Mutual Assistance Pact with the USA and Britain and began receiving a wide variety of arms including 140 de Havilland Mosquitos of different marks and 150 Republic F-47D Thunderbolts, resulting in a very substantial air force – easily the strongest in the unstable Balkan region at that time.*

The Thunderbolts stayed operational with the Jugoslovensko Ratno Vazduhoplovstvo well into the early 1960s, serving alongside much newer equipment such as the Canadair Sabre

ABOVE LEFT *The completed Thunderbolt was registered NX1345B and made its first post-restoration test flights from Minter Field during 1993 with Tiger Destefani doing the honours. The aircraft is owned and operated by the Museum of Flying at Santa Monica, and is seen in company with a new-build Yak-3 at the museum's Mojave Airport facility. The size of the P-47 is immediately apparent in this 8 September 1994 view, as it towers over Yak-3 NX915LP, which was purchased by Sir Tim Wallis and is now flying in New Zealand*

BELOW LEFT *Alan Preston flying NX1345B on 30 September 1993 near Minter Field. 'Let's get this photo flight over with', said Preston over the radio. 'I'm up to my ankles in avgas.' A fuel leak had pumped high octane into the cockpit and the flight was quickly, and safely, concluded so that repairs could be undertaken*

ABOVE *Fuel leak repaired, Preston is seen back in the air with NX1345B on 19 February 1994 over the Malibu beaches. Like most other currently flying Thunderbolts, this aircraft has had its turbosupercharger removed. The turbosupercharger, located in the bottom of the rear fuselage, was something of an Achilles Heel for the P-47, being prone to catching fire in flight. Since civilian P-47s are not operated at high altitudes, the need for the unit is obviated.*

OVERLEAF *Two of World War 2's most famous, and effective, fighters are seen in formation on 21 April 1995, with Tiger Destefani flying the Thunderbolt and Robert Converse piloting his North American P-51D Mustang. Both fighters wear the distinctive black and yellow chequers of the 353rd FG, who traded their P-47s for P-51s in October 1944. The 'LH' codes denote the 350th FS*

BIG ASS BIRD II

Over the lush fields of Geneseo, New York, Jeff Ethell forms a beautifully restored Thunderbolt with the National Warplane Museum's Twin Beech camera plane on 21 August 1993. P-47D-40-RA USAAF s/n 44-90368 was accepted by the Air Force on 8 May 1945 – VE-Day. The Thunderbolt was not sent to an overseas unit but stayed Stateside, operating with various training units. Surplus to postwar USAAF requirements, it was transferred to the Fuerza Aerea Venezolana during 1947.

Venezuela received its first six P-47s through US military aid on 28 August 1947, but two aircraft were almost immediately lost in fatal accidents so an agreement was reached for the supply of a further 22 Thunderbolts that had been in storage at Tinker AFB, Oklahoma. A contract was issued with Temco for the repair and refurbishment of the fighters and a number were duly flown to Miami for work, with the first group of four arriving in Venezuela in June 1949. Ferry flights continued, but were not uneventful, one pilot bailing out of his stricken aircraft. FAV peak Thunderbolt strength was 24 aircraft in April 1950.

In FAV service the 'T-Bolts' were given full US support, with the help of the USAF advisory team stationed in that country. However, parts began to become a problem, illustrating just how efficiently the US government scrapped its huge fleet of wartime aircraft. Also, Britain was making a strong play to sell its aircraft in Latin America, and, in what was perhaps a play on Latino machismo, a deal was struck that saw de Havilland Vampires sold to Venezuela, and by the end of 1951 only eight P-47s were still airworthy. As the number of British jets increased, the FAV phased out P-47 operations in 1954.

Some of the surviving eight aircraft must have been scrapped because in the early 1970s, as the warbird movement grew, various collectors started trying to get the FAV's four remaining P-47s. In 1986, French collector Jean Salis traded a replica Caudron G-III to the FAV museum for P-47D s/n 44-90368, and the fighter was crated and shipped to La Ferte-Alais near Paris

ABOVE Jean Salis did not remain the owner of '368 for very long since, in 1987, he sold the aircraft to Charles Osborne, who shipped it to the Blue Sky Aviation facility at Clark County Airport, Sellersburg, Indiana. The aircraft was broken down for restoration, and it was discovered that many vital parts were missing so a search began for the bits and pieces, and those that could not be found were remanufactured.

Osborne wanted to make the aircraft as original as possible so lots of wartime equipment including eight deactivated .50 cal Brownings and ammunition belts, armour plating, bomb shackles and a gunsight were added during the rebuild. However, the original Curtiss Electric propeller was replaced with a Hamilton Standard unit

LEFT The gun and magazine bay doors are cranked open to reveal a full warload of .50 Brownings and suitable belted ammunition. Few warbirds flying today can boast a similar weapons fit

ABOVE *Piloting N4747P during a recent Batavia shoot was John Davidson, whose usual mount is a Cessna Citation which he operates out of Louisville, Kentucky. BIG ASS BIRD II is the only fighter he has ever flown, but this didn't stop him handling the machine in a slick fashion during the air-to-air sortie*

RIGHT *The original BIG ASS BIRD was a 'T-Bolt' flown by Howard M Park who, during World War 2, logged 356 hours 40 minutes of P-47 time during more than 160 combat missions. In the process, Park won the DFC, 18 Oak Leaf Clusters to his Air Medal, two Purple Hearts, six campaign stars on his ETO ribbon and two Presidential Unit Citations. He was assigned a new P-47D on 7 July 1944 and crewchief Tom Menning decided to name the fighter for what it looked like – a 'Big Ass Bird'.*

On 29 September 1944 the machine was heavily hit by a flight of Messerschmitt Bf 109Gs, bur Park managed to crash behind American lines and was taken to a hospital, where 22 shell fragments were removed from his body. On return to combat he received P-47D s/n 44-32773 which was promptly named BIG ASS BIRD II. However, an Episcopalian

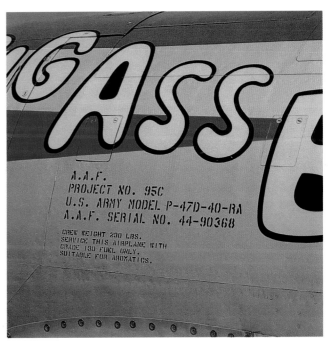

chaplain was offended by the name and complained to Park's CO, who ordered it to be removed. Ironically, Park became an Episcopalian priest after the war and, as of this writing, is still serving the faithful

Yank's unique M-model

ABOVE *Late evening sun on 22 December 1993 highlights YP-47M-RE USAAF s/n 42-27386 belonging to Yank's Air Museum, Chino, California. The P-47M was powered with a Pratt & Whitney R-2800-57 that could churn out a maximum of 2800 horsepower via a paddle-blade Curtiss Electric propeller. The variant was designed to give the P-47 a boost in speed to combat new German fighters, but it was at a price since at full power the -57 was gobbling an astonishing 330 gallons per hour!*

Only 130 P-47Ms were built, and the 56th FG received virtually the entire production run, but trouble soon followed. What worked under hasty factory conditions did not work in combat, and the pilots of the M-models were horrified to find their engines stopping completely or cutting in and out once they reached cruising altitude. Other engine problems

began to manifest themselves, including corrosion and low cylinder head temperatures which affected the correct operation of the engine. These problems soon grew to nightmare proportions when it became obvious that every P-47Ms operated by the 56th was stricken.

Ignition leads were suspect and were replaced with a different type, but the problem did not go away. Airflow to the cylinders was modified so that the heads could heat to the most efficient temperatures, and it was also discovered that the sensitive engine/turbosupercharger controls were not being correctly operated, so additional training for the pilots was required, along with some modifications. Eventually plagued by too many problems, all M-models had their engines changed

RIGHT *Detail view of the YP-47M showing the gunsight, armour glass and armour plating and the rear view mirror. After the end of the war, Republic apparently kept this machine for a while, before selling the dismantled aircraft to Bill Odum in 1947. Odum was making a name for himself in long-range flights, using aircraft as diverse as a Beech Bonanza and Douglas Invader. The P-47 was registered NX4477N and work began on modifying the aircraft for a long-distance attempt*

Odum wanted to use the YP-47M for a projected around-the-world flight, and had it gutted of all military equipment, and then relocated other components such as the turbo oil tank to make more space in the fuselage. He wanted to add more fuselage fuel for the flight and he also wetted the wings. The aircraft was entered in the 1947 Bendix cross-country race as the Reynolds Bombshell, race no 42.

Mechanical problems kept it out of the running, and the fighter was acquired by Earl Reinert of Chicago, who was a dealer in surplus military aircraft and parts. He was selling P-47 parts to Third World countries and, according to Stan Hoefler – the man responsible for Yank's outstanding aircraft restorations – 'Earl removed various components for his surplus business and stored the aircraft outside for its entire life. When we got it in 1985, it was in truly terrible shape. It looked like some one had unloaded the fuselage by merely dumping it out of a truck. The whole right side was smashed. There was lots of corrosion and we had to use new high-tech methods to repair the wing spar.

'I had two Argentine brothers working on the project and they are extremely skilled with metal and did an excellent job repairing the fuselage, as well as reskinning the wings and elevators. Almost all interior components had been removed, so we had to start a search for all the bits we needed. Without a doubt, this aircraft was our biggest challenge because of its condition, and that's why it took 13,000 man hours to get it back into flying condition'.

The YP-47M is now registered N27385, but will not be flown for a while due to expansion at the Yank's Air Museum, as well as the backlog of restorations

Brazilian Beauties

ABOVE *During 1988 four ex-Forca Aerea Brasileira P-47Ds were transferred to Chino to be put up for sale. These aircraft were the last remaining
examples of Brazil's once mighty Thunderbolt force, and the aircraft were
in varying degrees of preservation. One is seen here partially assembled at
Santa Monica on 15 April 1993, where it was being offered for sale.*

*Brazil had the distinction of flying Thunderbolts operationally
during World War 2 in the Italian campaign. The US and its Allies had*

*been pushing Latin American nations to enter the war on their side since
the pre-war German presence had been quite strong in many of these
countries. Brazil declared war on the Axis on 22 August 1942, mainly
because of U-boat attacks on surface shipping inside the Brazilian Security
Zone. Accordingly, this declaration opened up the pipeline of American
supplies and 350 Brazilian personnel were sent to undergo training with
the 30th FS to ready them for operational combat deployment. In 1944, the*

unit began training with the P-47 as 1 Grupo de Aviacao de Caca – they operated with distinction from 1944 with the Twelfth Air Force in Italy

RIGHT *The four aircraft imported to the US during 1988 were 44-90103, 44-90294, 45-49346 and 45-49406. After the end of the war, Brazil had its 26 combat veteran P-47s shipped home from Italy, while others were supplied from the USAAF to create Latin America's strongest fighter force – these were kept at a high state of readiness, although spares were hard to find. With paint stripped off, the vertical tail of the P-47 reveals its post-1947 USAF designation and a serial not matching any of the four given for the imported aircraft – perhaps this was a replacement spare part?*

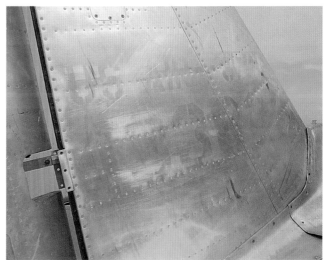

LEFT *Work underway on the Yank's Air Museum's second Thunderbolt, P-47D USAAF s/n 45-49346. This aircraft was made available to Brazil under the Military Defense Assistance Program and sent to Temco Aircraft, where it was upgraded to F-47D-40 status before being sent to Brazil where it operated until being struck off charge in 1967 and placed as a monument in Sao Paulo. Transferred to Chino in 1988, it was purchased by Yank's in 1991 and registered N3152D*

BELOW LEFT *When photographed during November 1994, a great deal of work had been done on Yank's second Thunderbolt. At the time it was planned to trade the completed aircraft for a fighter type that the collection was missing. In Brazilian service, as parts became more critical, the Thunderbolt was finally withdrawn in 1957/58, by which time about 40 were still in the FAB's inventory. Some of these aircraft were transferred to museum/memorial use, while a few others soldiered on within the air force as instructional airframes*

BELOW *Right wing panel of '346 opened up, showing the original zinc chromate interior finish and overall lack of corrosion*

BELOW *Some of the original equipment for the Browning machine guns was still in place when the gun bay of '346 was photographed. When in Forca Aerea Brasileira service, the Thunderbolt was serialled 4191*

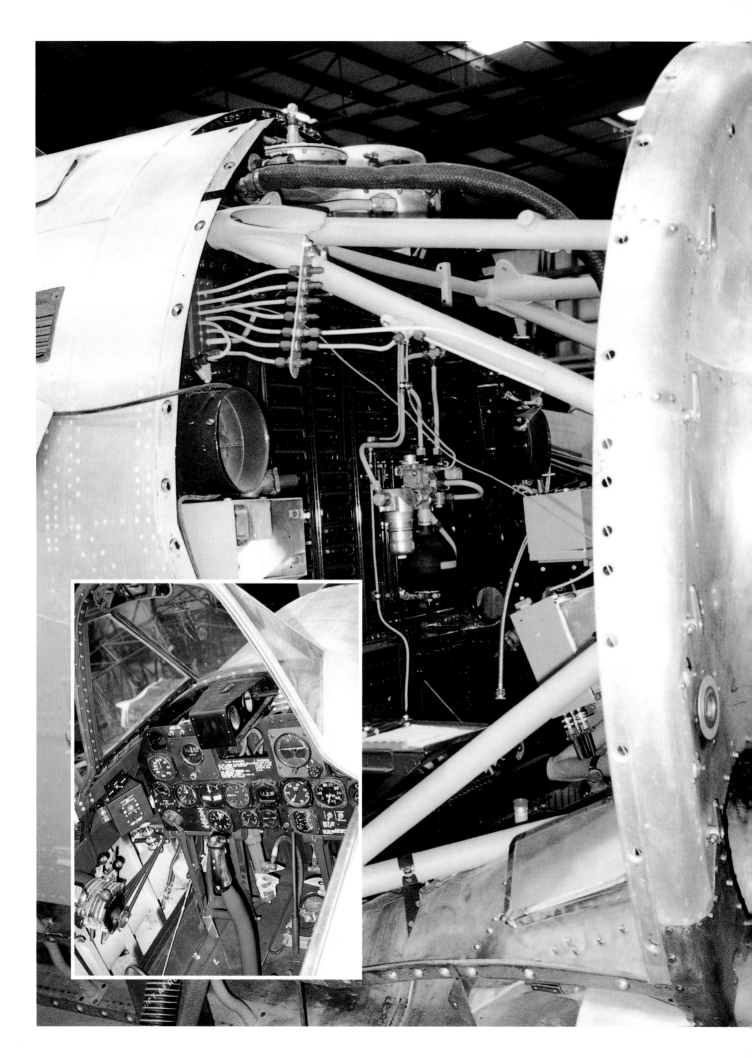

LEFT *The fuselage of '346 in its jig, showing the quality of restoration for various components mounted on the firewall*

LEFT INSET *As with other Yank's aircraft, '346 is being restored to appear as it did when it left the factory. 'We don't want any chrome, extra anodizing or any customising', states Yank's restoration director Stan Hoefler*

RIGHT *Partially restored cockpit of '346 illustrating the throttle and trim controls*

BELOW *Inside the spacious fuselage (minus the turbosupercharger!) and looking towards the tail cone, illustrating control rods and wires and the general thoroughness of the restoration carried out by Yank's*

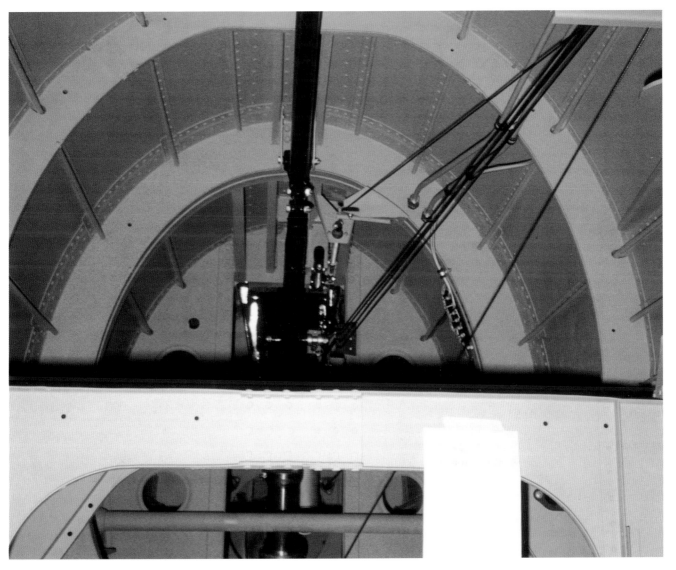

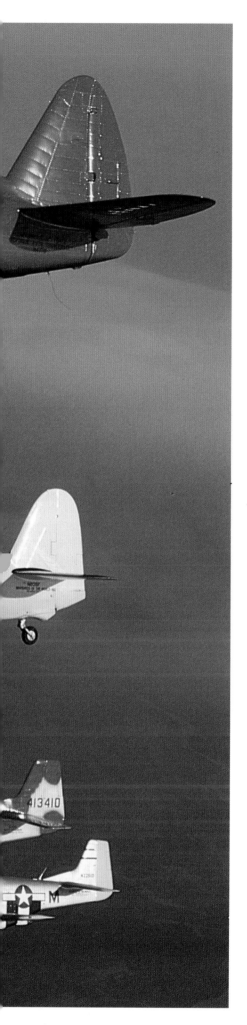

Last of the N-models

ABOVE *Silver-painted P-47N-15-RE USAAF s/n 44-89436 N47TB is seen taxying at Harlingen prior to take-off during October 1976. The Fuerza Aerea de la Guardia Nacional de Nicaragua received six P-47Ns (or F-47Ns as they were known at that time) for rather nefarious purposes.*

During the early 1950s, the CIA was having a pretty good time in Latin America since there were no 'watch guard' organisations in place. In order to depose the new ruler of Guatemala, who was deemed as being possibly unfriendly to US interests, the CIA set up Operation Success, part of which included the transfer of numerous military aircraft. Six F-47Ns were transferred to Nicaragua – not for Nicaraguan use, but rather for CIA operations.

These aircraft were from the Puerto Rican Air National Guard (PRANG) and were flown in a variety of outlandish missions against Guatemala – at this time the latter's fighter force consisted of two Boeing P-26 Peashooters! For its part in the collapse of Guatemala, Nicaragua received the survivors of the original six F-47s, plus replacements from the PRANG in order to field six F-47Ns

LEFT *By October 1977 the CAF's P-47N had received some adornment in the form of blue and black bands. In an unfortunate example of warbird attrition, the two P-51s and solitary Sea Fury illustrated here have since crashed, although the Mustangs were eventually rebuilt. Sadly, the P-47N was also the subject of several accidents but was rebuilt back to flying condition after each incident.*

Once the FAN had received its 'force' of six F-47Ns, little flying was actually done, but they still managed to write off three of the aircraft. In 1962, CAF member Dick Disney travelled to Nicaragua and struck a deal to obtain aircraft GN 71, the best of the three remaining F-47s – it was ferried to Texas to join the CAF's fleet as N478C. The other two F-47Ns were purchased by Will Martin and flown back to the US, but both crashed and were destroyed on their way 'back home', fortunately without loss of life

ABOVE LEFT *The big, powerful, lines of the P-47N are illustrated over Breckenridge, Texas, during May 1990. Over the years, the aircraft has gone through several CAF 'sponsors', who have helped maintain and keep the P-47N flying. Sponsor Linda Finch is seen here at the controls of N47TB during May 1990.*

Although American female pilots did not fly the Thunderbolt in combat during World War 2, WASP pilots did fly P-47Ns (and virtually every other type of combat aircraft) from factories and maintenance bases to operational units. Currently, Finch is rebuilding a rare Lockheed Model 10E in order to recreate Amelia Earhart's final ill-fated trans-global flight

LEFT *Undersurface view of N47TB shows the location of the turbosupercharger and engine exhausts to advantage. Also, the extended wing of the N-model is clearly evident, along with the more rectangular wing tips. Designed specifically for Pacific operations, the P-47N had its fuel capacity increased by 200 gallons, while the tread of the landing gear was*

increased by 24 inches. Since the aircraft was going to flying long distances, an autopilot was added to help decrease the pilot's work load. All the extra weight meant that, even with increased wing area, the take-off distance increased by 1000 ft

ABOVE *N47TB touching down at Breckenridge on 28 May 1993 in a camouflage scheme never worn by a P-47N. With the N-model, the Thunderbolt became World War 2's heaviest single-engine fighter, weighing in at over 21,000 lbs.*

The first unit to get the P-47N was the 318th FG on the small island of Ie Shima, only 325 miles from the Japanese Home Islands – Ie Shima is perhaps best known as the location where famed journalist Ernie Pyle was killed by Japanese sniper fire.

The N-model was soon causing havoc on what was left of the Japanese air arm, with two 318th P-47N pilots becoming instant aces when they each destroyed five Japanese aircraft during one mission

The Peruvian Connection

RIGHT *Suitably attired in a cowboy hat, a CAF pilot undertakes a ground power run on the P&W R-2800 installed in P-47D USAAF s/n 45-49205 N47DE at Galveston on 19 May 1973. In 1947 the Fuerza Aerea del Peru began receiving its first US-supplied P-47s. Peru had operated 30 Curtiss P-36Gs during World War 2, and had experienced pilots that could transition to the powerful Thunderbolt.*

The initial 25 P-47Ds saw restricted flying since parts were hard to come by, and it was judged that by 1949 only five of the surviving 23 P-47s were operational. Accordingly, a search for more parts and airframes was undertaken, and 25 more were acquired, along with spare parts. In FAP service N47DE was FAP 457, it having been received by Temco as a TF-47D-30-RA and upgraded to F-47-40 specs before shipment to Peru

LEFT *Peru became the largest supplier of Thunderbolts for American warbird buffs when, in 1967, six aircraft and 50,000 lbs of spare parts were purchased by auto and aircraft collector Ed Jurist of Nyack, New York. The aircraft were shipped by sea aboard the SS* Rosaldina *to Brownsville, Texas, where they arrived on 5 September 1969.*

The fighters were then trucked to CAF headquarters at Harlingen where, in a deal worked out with Jurist, they were assembled, 'IRANed' (Inspect and Repair As Necessary) and then flown. In the early 1970s, the sky around Harlingen was host to the amazing sight of six of the ex-Peruvian aircraft flying in formation.

N47DF was ex-FAP 549 and was another of the Thunderbolts upgraded by Temco to D-40 standards. N47DF was photographed at Palomar, California, on 15 January 1974 in the markings of the 354th FG's UNADILLA KILLA

ABOVE *Collector David Tallichet pulled off an amazing warbird coup in 1975 when he purchased Jurist's six Thunderbolts, de Havilland Mosquito, Supermarine Spitfire Mk IX and other aircraft, and had the majority transferred to his Chino base of operations, then known as the Military Aircraft Restoration Corp. N47DF was to have numerous problems, crashing on take-off on 3 July 1980 at Barstow, California.*

The aircraft was moved around to several rebuilding locations and finally put on loan to the Liberal Air Museum, Kansas. During October 1990 the P-47 was being flown back to Chino when it was damaged in a crash-landing near Flagstaff, Arizona. Although looking complete when seen at Chino on 17 June 1992, N47DF was far from being airworthy

ABOVE RIGHT *During 1994 N47DF was sold and moved to nearby Klaers Aviation at Rialto Airport. At that location Bill Klaers, Alan Wojciak and Bob Lumbard tore into the disassembled airframe and found it to be in worse condition than originally thought.*

Not to be easily defeated, the trio decided to rebuild N47DF back to 'GI condition', and to include a fully-functioning turbosupercharger. Here, Bob Lumbard examines his handiwork after installing a newly-blown canopy in its frame

RIGHT *Alan Wojciak pulls off masking tape after painting the national insignia on the side of N47DF*

Right *The first post-restoration flight of N47DF was delayed after a loaned chin cowling was taken back by its owner, forcing the trio to make their own from original plans. This is a complex unit that houses a substantial amount of ducting – this predicament illustrates just how hard it is to find original P-47 parts nowadays*

Below *Overhauled P&W R-2800 mated to the Curtiss Wright propeller and 'mini spinner' prop hub*

Above *Each of the propeller blades on N47DF boasts an authentic Curtiss decal, thus denoting the restored airscrew's origin*

Trio of Thunderbolt rebuilders – from left, Bill Klaers, Bob Lumbard and Alan Wojciak – on the wing of the nearly-completed N47DF. This project has consumed thousands of man hours, but will result in one of the most original of all surviving Thunderbolts

ABOVE LEFT *Since World War 2 only three Thunderbolts have flown in unlimited air races, and P-47D USAAF s/n 45-49167/N47DB was one of that trio. Last operating in Peru as FAP 116, the aircraft was given a 353rd FG paint scheme and flown by Lefty Gardner at the 1974 Reno National Air Races. It was then grounded and displayed at one of Dave Tallichet's restaurants at St Petersburg, Florida, where it was subsequently damaged in a storm. N47DB was eventually rebuilt and traded to the USAF Museum in 1981*

LEFT *With portions of its previous Peruvian Air Force markings showing through its coat of World War 2-style paint, P-47D-40-RA USAAF s/n 45-49181, ex-FAP 115, N47DC is seen at Van Nuys, California, during December 1977, prior to a repaint for new owner Lester Friend, who registered the 'T-Bolt' N159LF. In 1979, the aircraft was sold to the Kalamazoo Aviation History Museum in Michigan and completely rebuilt, emerging with the new registration N444SU*

ABOVE *P-47D-40-RA USAAF 45-49192, ex-FAP 119, N47DD looking rather tired at Harlingen during October 1975 (some of the original Peruvian markings are showing through the paint). After purchase by David Tallichet, this aircraft was sold, but was then heavily damaged after crashing on take-off from Tulsa, Oklahoma, while on a ferry flight to new owner Robin Collard on 9 February 1980. The wreckage passed through the hands of several owners until purchased by Stephen Grey, and some of the remains were used to build up static display Thunderbolt 45-49295, which was completed in mid-1995 for the RAF Museum*

PREVIOUS PAGES *By October 1979 Thunderbolt N47DE was certainly looking a bit worse for wear. David Tallichet stored the aircraft at his Barstow, California, facility after purchase from Ed Jurist, but then sold the fighter to British warbird collector Doug Arnold in May 1979 for addition to the latter's growing collection of vintage aircraft then based at Blackbushe, England. Pete Regina flew the aircraft to Van Nuys and began going through the big fighter to make sure everything was safe for the long ferry flight to England. Part of this inspection and repair process included the installation of two huge drop tanks to satisfy the thirst of the R-2800 on the long flight. Dave Zeuschel is seen test flying the aircraft from Chino prior to the ferry flight*

BELOW *Some of the wreckage of N47DD USAAF s/n 45-49192 was combined with a spare P-47N fuselage and other parts to create a 'new' NX47DD that was owned by Jon Ward. Work was carried out by Glen Necessary at Truckee, California, before the project was moved to Agua Dulce, also in California, where restoration continued in a large garage. In 1985 the aircraft was acquired by Stephen Grey and transported to Fighter Rebuilders for completion. Work is seen being carried out on NX47DD at Chino during December 1985 as it is disassembled for shipment to England and the Stephen Grey collection*

LEFT *Zeuschel banks N47DE against the harsh backdrop of the San Gabriel Mountains near Chino. Mike Wright was chosen as ferry pilot for the epic journey, and he and N47DE arrived safely at Blackbushe on 11 November 1979. The aircraft was rarely, if ever, flown, but received the British civil registration G-BLZW. In 1985 the aircraft was sold to Stephen Grey, who in turn quickly sold it to Bob Pond on 17 December 1985. The P-47 is seen back at Chino during 1986 undergoing an overhaul by Steve Hinton's Fighter Rebuilders*

LEFT *Steve Hinton flying the 'new' NX47DD near Madera, California, during August 1985, shortly after the aircraft's first post-restoration test flight from Chino. After flying off the required number of hours, Fighter Rebuilders crated the Thunderbolt and shipped the hybrid airframe to Duxford, where it arrived on 22 January 1986*

LEFT *Once re-assembled in the UK, the aircraft flew for a brief time in its 'US' scheme, before the red cowl band was replaced by an authentic 78th FG chequered nose and the fuselage code painted over with fully-blown invasion stripes. In this unique view Carl Schofield is at the controls of N47DD, with the Martlet IV (actually a Wildcat) being flown by Pete Kynsey. The photo was taken off the Normandy coast during the 50th anniversary year of the Allied invasion of occupied Europe in 1994 (John Dibbs)*

BELOW *High above a thick cloud layer, The Fighter Collection's Thunderbolt shows its classic wing form to advantage, with TFC regular Hoof Proudfoot in cockpit on this occasion (John Dibbs)*

LEFT *The nickname* No Guts – No Glory! *was originally carried by P-47D 42-26671 at Duxford in 1944. This machine was the mount of Lt Col Ben Mayo, CO of the 82nd FS, and also a five-kill ace. The Fighter Collection's P-47 is a spirited performer at many a British and European airshow during the display season, arguably being the most flown Thunderbolt in the world today (John Dibbs)*

ABOVE *During the summer of 1986, Chino Airport could boast of having five P-47s in residence, although not all were flyable. NX47RP carries the name* BIG CHIEF *on its cowling, certainly an appropriate name for the Thunderbolt*

LEFT *When Fighter Rebuilders finished overhauling P-47D USAAF s/n 45-49205 for Bob Pond, the aircraft was re-registered NX47RP. Here, Steve Hinton is seen bringing the freshly-painted fighter in for a bit of close formation work during July 1986*

RIGHT *Warbirds continually need maintenance, and here some last minute brake work is performed on NX47RP before a July 1986 test hop*

Appendices

LOCKHEED P-38 LIGHTNING FIGHTER VARIANTS

XP-38
Highly advanced long-range fighter with two Allison V-12 engines, propellers rotating towards fuselage pod and with provision for four .50 cal machine guns and one 23 mm cannon in the nose, but these were not installed. The aircraft quickly set records when first flown during January 1939, but the single prototype was destroyed in a crash on 11 February. Highly polished metal finish. Lockheed Model number 022-64-01.

YP-38-LO
Thirteen pre-production service test examples (Model 122-62-02). Most were delivered in natural metal and sprayed alumilesnum finish. The Allison engines were equipped with outward rotating propellers. Armament consisted of two .50 cal and two .30 cal machine guns and one 37 mm cannon.

P-38-LO
The first production version (Model 222-62-02) with 30 built. Limilested armour protection and four .50 cal machine guns and one 37 mm cannon. Most, if not all, were delivered in Olive Drab and Neutral Grey camouflage. Most aircraft used for training.

XP-38A-LO
Experimental conversion of P-38-LO s/n 40-762 to test a pressurised cockpit (Model 622-62-10).

P-38D-LO
Model 222-62-08. Basically the same as P-38-LO but with more mileslitary equipment added, including self-sealing tanks and extra armour. Flares were also added along with a low-pressure oxygen system. Thirty-six were built, all delivered in Olive Drab and Neutral Grey camouflage.

P-38E-LO
Basically the same as the P-38D but the hydraulic system had been reworked. The 37 mm cannon was replaced with a more reliable 20 mm Hispano weapon. Some aircraft had Curtiss Electric propellers and most had the SCR274N radio. A total of 210 built, some converted to F-4-1-LO.

P-38F-LO
Model 222-60-09. Variants of the F received new model numbers: F-1 was Model 222-60-15; F-5 was 222-60-12 and other models became 322-60-19. Pylons inboard of engines for the carriage of 2000 lb bombs or external fuel tanks. F-15 saw introduction of a modified Fowler flap.

P-38G-LO
Basically the same as the F except for new engines (V-1710-51/55) and revised internal radio gear. The G was Model 222-68-12 (G-13 and G-15 were Model 322-68-19 – RAF Lightning Mk IIs never delivered).

P-38H-LO
Model 422-81-20. Two Allison V-1710-89/91 engines equipped with automatic oil radiator gills for improved cooling. The underwing carriage of weapons or fuel was increased to 3200 lb. 601 built and 128 converted as F-5C-LO.

P-38J-LO
Model 422-81-14 covered J-1 and J-5, 422-81-22 the J-10, 522-81-22 the J-15 and -20, and 522-87-23 the J-25. The J introduced the most distinctive physical change in the Lightning series in the form of large chin radiators for much improved engine cooling. All J variants, except the J-1, had greatly increased fuel capacity, thus allowing them to escort bombers both to and from targets in Germany. With the J-10, a flat, optically correct, bullet-proof windshield was finally introduced. The J-25 had totally new dive brakes and the power-assisted ailerons. The majority of these aircraft were delivered to the USAAF in natural metal finish. Total of 2970 built, including F-5E/F-5F photo variants.

P-38K-LO
One aircraft only, Model 422-85-22. Basically the same as P-38J, but Allison V-1710-75/77 engines equipped with paddle-blade propellers. Earlier XP-38K-LO was a P-38E conversion.

P-38L-LO/VN
Model 422-87-23. Basically the same as P-38J, but with V-1710-111/113 engines and the landing light now in the port wing. 3801 J-LOs built, 113 L-VNs built at the Vultee plant. Connections for ten 5-in rockets under wing.

P-38M-LO
Model 522-87-23 was a conversion of the basic P-38L into a two-seat night fighter (75 built), with radar mounted under nose in pod. Solid black finish.

OTHER VARIANTS

XFO-1

Five F-5B-LOs assigned to the US Navy in North Africa and given BuNos 012109 through 012112.

F-4-l-LO

Unarmed photo-recon variant of the P-38E, equipped with four K17 cameras and an autopilot. Type was designated Model 222-62-13 and 99 aircraft were numbered with serials 41-2098/2099, 2121/2156, 2158/2171, 2172/2218, 2220. F-4A-1-LO used the P-38F as the basic airframe and 20 were built (41-2362/2381). Most were delivered in special blue-grey 'haze' camouflage.

F-5A

Modified P-38G for photo recon. F-5A-3 Model 222-68-16 s/ns 42-12767/12789. F-5A-10 Model 222-68-16 s/ns 42-12967/12986, 42-13067/13126, 42-13267/13326. Most were delivered in 'haze' camouflage.

F-5B

Modification of P-38J-10-LO for photo-recon. Designated Model 422-81-21 with 200 built, s/ns 42-76312/67401, 42-68192/68301.

F-5C

P-38H modification for photo recon as Model 222-68-16 with 123 built.

XF-5D

Model 222-68-16. Rebuild of F-5A-10-LO modified with Plexiglas nose cone and prone observer's position. Two .50 cal machine guns and a vertical camera fitted.

F-5E

P-38J photo-recon modification. F-5E-2-LO (P-38J-15-LO) was Model 422-81-22 with 100 built. F-5E-3-LO Model 522-87-23 was a conversion of 105 J-25-LOs. F-5E-4-LO Model 422-87-23 was a conversion of 500 L-1-LOs.

F-5F-3-LO

Model 422-87-23 photo-recon version of P-38L-5-LO

F-5G-6-LO

Model 422-87-23 basically the same as the F-5F-3-LO, but with different cameras.

Model 322

Lightning for the RAF. 243 Mk Is ordered (AE978/999, AF100/220), but just one was delivered, the rest being taken over by the USAAF as the P-322 and flown as trainers. An order for 524 Mk. IIs (AF221/744) was cancelled.

LOCKHEED LIGHTNING SERIAL NUMBERS

XP-38-LO 37-457

YP-38-LO 39-689 through 39-701

P-38-LO 40-744 through 40-773

XP-38A-LO 40-762

P-38D-LO 40-774 through 40-809

P-38E-LO 41-1983 through 41-2097, 41-2100 through 41-2120, 41-2172, 41-2219, 41-2221 through 41-2292

P-38F-LO 41-2293 through 41-2321

P-38F-1-LO 41-2322

P-38F-LO 41-2323 through 41-2358

P-38F-1-LO 41-2359 through 41-2361

P-38F-LO 41-2382 through 41-2386

P-38F-1-LO 41-2387

P-38F-LO 41-2388 through 41-2392

P-38F-1-LO 41-7486 through 41-7496

P-38F-1-LO 41-7497

P-38F-LO 41-7498 through 41-7513

P-38F-1-LO 41-7514 through 41-7515

P-38F-LO 41-7516 through 41-7524

P-38F-1-LO 41-7525

P-38F-LO 41-7526 through 41-7530

P-38F-1-LO 41-7531

P-38F-LO 41-7532 through 41-7534

P-38F-1-LO 41-7535

P-38F-LO 41-7536 through 41-7538

P-38F-1-LO 41-7539 through 41-7541

P-38F-LO 41-7542 through 41-7543

P-38F-1-LO 41-7544

P-38F-LO 41-7545 through 41-7547

P-38F-1-LO 41-7548 through 41-7550

P-38F-LO 41-7551

P-38F-1-LO 41-7552 through 41-7680

P-38F-5-LO 41-12567 through 42-12666

P-38J-5-LO 42-67102 through 42—67311

P-38J-10-LO 42-67402 through 42-68191

P-38J-15-LO 42-103939 through 42-104428, 43-28248 through 44-2904, 44-23509 through 44-23208

P-38J-20-LO 44-23209 through 44-23558

P-38J-25-LO 44-23209 through 44-23768

XP-38K-LO 41-1983

P-38K-1-LO 42-13558

P-38L-1-LO 44-23769 through 44-25058

P-38L-5-LO 44-25059 through 44-27258, 44-53008 through 44-53327

P-38L-5-VN 43-50226 through 43-30338

P-38M-LO 44-25237 (converted by Lockheed from P-38L-5-LO to serve as a prototype for this nightfighter variant – other serials chosen at random)

Stephen Grey enjoys himself in his recently-restored P-38J on the spring of 1992 over Cambridgeshire. The Lightning wears the markings of eight-kill ace Jack Ilfrey, who nicknamed his Lightning HAPPY JACK'S GO BUGGY – the 1st FG's markings fitted in nicely with the natural metal finish in which the aircraft had been delivered. Ilfrey went on to fly P-51Ds with the 20th FG. The Fighter Collection's P-38J was immediately booked into many airshows in Europe and Britain, where the type had rarely been seen (John Dibbs)

LOCKHEED LIGHTNING SPECIFICATIONS

XP-38

Span 52 ft
Length 37 ft 10 in
Height 12 ft 10 in
Wing Area 327.5 sq ft
Empty Weight 11,507 lb
Loaded Weight 15,416 lb
Max Speed 413 mph
Cruise Speed n/a
Ceiling 38,000 ft
Rate of Climb 20,000 ft in 6.5 minutes
Range n/a
Powerplants Allison V-1710-11 of 1150 hp

YP-38

Span 52 ft
Length 37 ft 10 in
Height 9 ft 10 in
Wing Area 327.5 sq ft
Empty Weight 11,171 lb
Loaded Weight 14,348 lb
Max Speed 405 mph
Cruise Speed 330 mph
Ceiling 38,000 ft
Rate of Climb 3300 fpm
Range 650 miles
Powerplants Allison V-1710-27/29 of
    1150 hp

P-38

Dimensions as YP-38
Empty Weight 11,670 lb
Loaded Weight 15,340 lb
Max Speed 390 mph
Cruise Speed 310 mph
Ceiling n/a
Rate of Climb 3200 fpm
Range 825 to 1500 miles
Powerplants Allison V-1710-27/29 of
    1150 hp

P-38D

Dimensions as YP-38
Empty Weight 11,780 lb
Loaded Weight 15,500 lb
Max Speed 390 mph
Cruise Speed 300 mph
Ceiling 39,000 ft
Rate of Climb 20,000 ft in 8 minutes
Range 400 to 975 miles
Powerplants Allison V-1710-27/29 of 1150 hp

P-38E

Dimensions as YP-38
Empty Weight 11,880 lb
Loaded Weight 15,482 lb
Max Speed 395 mph
Cruise Speed n/a
Rate of Climb n/a
Range 500 miles
Powerplant Allison V-1710-27/29 of
    1150 hp

P-38F

Dimensions as YP-38
Empty Weight 12,265 lb
Loaded Weight 18,000 lb
Max Speed 395 mph
Cruise Speed 305 mph
Rate of Climb 20,000 ft in 8.8 minutes
Range 350 to 1900 miles
Powerplants Allison V-1710-49/53 of
    1325 hp

P-38G

Dimensions as YP-38
Empty Weight 12,200 lb
Loaded Weight 19,800 lb
Max Speed 400 mph
Cruise Speed 340 mph
Rate of Climb 20,000 ft in 8.5 minutes
Range 275 to 2400 miles
Powerplants Allison V-1710-51/55 of
    1325 hp

P-38H

Dimensions as YP-38
Empty Weight 12,380 lb
Loaded Weight 20,300 lb
Max Speed 402 mph
Cruise Speed 300 mph
Rate of Climb 2600 fpm
Range 300 to 2400 miles
Powerplants Allison V-1710-89/91 of
    1425 hp

P-38J

Dimensions as YP-38
Empty Weight 12,780 lb
Loaded Weight 21,600 lb
Max Speed 414 mph
Cruise Speed 290 mph
Rate of Climb 20,000 ft in 7 miles
Powerplants Allison V-1710-89/91 of
    1425 hp

P-38L

Dimensions as YP-38
Empty Weight 12,800 lb
Loaded Weight 21,600 lb
Max Speed 414 mph
Cruise Speed n/a
Rate of Climb 20,000 ft in 7 miles
Range 450 to 2625 miles
Powerplants Allison V-1710-111/173 of
    1425 hp

THUNDERBOLT VARIANTS

XP-47-RE

Republic project that did not pass beyond the initial design stage. It had a 1150 hp Allison V-1710-39 and was armed with .50 cal nose guns and four .30 cal guns in the wing. Assigned serial 40-3051, the aircraft eventually turned into the XP-47B-RE.

X-47A-RE

Same concept as above but with a lighter airframe and only nose guns retained. Serial 40-3052 was allotted but the project did not pass beyond the design stage.

XP-47B-RE

First of the Thunderbolts with Pratt & Whitney (P&W) XR-2800-2 of 2000 hp. The turbosupercharger was mounted in rear fuselage. Flew on 2 May 1941, but crashed and was destroyed on 8 August 1942. Bare metal finish. Many design changes during aircraft's life.

P-47B

Similar to prototype, but with many design detail changes including sliding canopy and metal-covered control surfaces. Genearl Electric (GE) A-13 turbosupercharger. Six or eight .50 cal guns could be carried. First example completed during December 1941. First five aircraft became pre-production test and evaluation machines. Production aircraft were assigned to 56th and 78th FGs. Delivered in Olive Drab and Neutral Grey standard camouflage.

P-47C

C-1-RE had R-2800-21 engine, six or eight .50 cal guns with 300 to 425 rpg, revised oxygen system, and A-17 turbosupercharger regulator. First C-1-RE completed on 14 September 1942. C-2-RE had metal-covered rudder and elevators, 128 built. C-5-RE just had radio and mast change – 362 built.

P-47D

D-1-RA – 114 built – was the first Thunderbolt constructed at the new Evansville (RA), Indiana, plant starting in December 1942. Similar to C-5-RE. D-1-RE had additional cowl flaps, more pilot armour, new radio and mast – 105 built. D-2-RA built at Evansville (200 aircraft), similar to the D-1-RE with minor improvements to fuel system – 100 D-3-RAs were built and were similar to D-2-RE. D-5-RE (300 built) similar to D-1-RE, but with modifications to fuel and hydraulic system. D-4-RA (200 built) was similar to D-5-RE. D-6-RE (350 built) was similar to D-1-RE, but had two-point shackles for a bomb or drop tank under the fuselage. D-10-RE (250 built) similar to D-1-RE with minor changes in hydraulic system and addition of GE C-23 turbosupercharger. D-11-RE (400 built) was equipped with a 2300 hp P&W R-2800-63 with water injection, while D-11-RA was similar to D-11-RE (250 built). D-15-RE (496 built) had wing stations for a bomb or drop tank under each wing panel and the increased payload, giving the ability to carry up to two 1000 lb bombs or three 500 lb bombs. The D-15-RA (157 built) was similar to the D-15-RE. The D-16-RE (254 built) was similar to the D-11-RE, but could only use 100/150 octane fuel. Only 29 D-16-RAs were built and they were similar to the D-16-RE. The D-20-RE (250 built) had a 2300 hp P&W R-2800-59, along with a raised tailwheel strut, GE ignition harness and other slight modifications. 187 D-20-RAs were built and were similar to the D-20-RE. The D-21-RE had manual water injection control, and was similar to the D-11-RE except that aircraft were delivered in natural-metal finish – 216 built. D-21-RA – 224 built – was basically the same as the D-21-RE. 850 D-22-REs built with a 13 ft Hamilton Standard paddle-blade propeller and A-23 turbosupercharger regulator. D-23-RA, 889 built, had a Curtiss Electric 13 ft paddle-blade propeller. The bubble canopy was introduced with the D-25-RE (385 built), which had increased oxygen supplies with repositioned integral equipment with increased fuel capacity (270 US gallons). D-26-RA (250 built) was similar to the D-25-RE. 615 D-27-REs were similar to the D-25-RE except for minor fuel system changes. D-28-RA (1028 built) was similar to the D-26-RA. 750 D-28-REs built, which were similar to the D-25-RE, but with a Curtiss paddle-blade prop. 800 D-30-REs were built, similar to the D-25-RE, but with rocket stubs for five HVARs under each wing panel. D-30-RA (1800 built) was similar to the D-30-RE. D-40-RA (9665 built) introduced a dorsal fin for increased stability.

XP-47E

USAAF s/n 41-6065 converted to have a pressurised cabin. Modified numerous times during test life. Fitted with an R-2800-21 and -59 with Curtiss Electric and Hamilton Standard propellers. Its performance was similar to that of the P-47B except for higher speeds with new engine and propeller, so production was not warranted.

XP-47F

USAAF s/n 415938 converted from P-47B to test new laminar flow wing. No armament. Lost in fatal crash on 14 October 1943.

P-47G

20 G-CU Thunderbolts were built by Curtiss of Buffalo, New York, with R-2800-21s and Curtiss Electric 12 ft 2 in propellers but were similar to the C-1-RE. First aircraft completed December 1942. 40 G-1-CU similar to the C-5-RE, 60 G-5-CU similar to D-1-RE, 80 G-10-CU identical to D-6-RE and 154 G-15-CU similar to D-11-RE were built. Most were assigned training roles.

XP-47H

S/n 42-23297 and 42-23298 were converted from D-15-RA airframes and modified for test work with the 2300 hp Chrysler XIV-2220-1.

XP-47J

S/n 43-46952 fitted with 2800 hp R-2800-57 and cooling fan in shortened nose with CH-5 turbosupercharger and many design detail changes. Armed with six .50 cal guns with 267 rpg. Project dropped when aircraft could not reach manufacturer's estimated top speed.

XP-47K

Last D-5-RE, s/n 42-8702, modified to test bubble canopy. Later tested bigger wing for P-47N.

XP-47L

Last D-20-RE, s/n 42-76614, modified into basically XP-47K version, but with design detail changes. Later served as test bed for R-2800-C engine.

P-47M

Three YP-47M-REs built to test 2800 hp P&W R-2800-14W and -57 engines with Curtiss Electric C642S-B40 13 ft diameter propellers with ability to carry six or eight .50 cal weapons with 267 rpg. YPs tested R-2800-C and related components. 130 M-1-RE higher-powered variants of the D-30-RE built and sent to 56th FG, where dorsal fins were fitted as field mod.

P-47N

XP-47N, converted D-27-RE, built with R-2800-57 and Curtiss Electric 13 ft propeller, unilever power control, CH-5 turbosupercharger and new long-range wing. New engine mount and cowling, design detail changes, 40 US gallon oil tank, and six/eight gun wing. 550 N-1-REs built with unilever power control dropped and replaced by automatic engine control unit and new ignition harness. Extra fuel in wing gave a total of 186 US gallons, and 300 US gallon drop tanks could be carried under each wing panel. 550 N-5-REs also built, basically similar to N-1-RE but with minor detail changes and addition of rocket launchers and AN/APS-11 tail warning radar and provision for GE C-1 autopilot. 200 N-15-REs built similar to N-1-RE except for addition of S-1 bomb rack and new K-14A/B gunsight, while automatic engine control was dropped. 200 N-20-REs built, similar to N-1-RE except for new radio and other minor changes. 149 N-20-RAs were similar to N-20-RE except for minor cockpit changes. 167 N-25-REs built, similar to N-1-RE except for installation of automatic engine controls, auto pilot, new cockpit floor and strengthened aileron to deflect blast from rocket firing. They were final Thunderbolts built on the Farmingdale line, which closed October 1945.

THUNDERBOLT SERIAL NUMBERS

XP-47A-RE 40-3052 *(cancelled)*
XP-47B-RE 40-3051
P-47B-RE 41-5895 through 41-6064
P-47C-RE 41-6067 through 41-6123
P-47C-1-RE 41-6066, 41-6124
    through 41-6177
P-47C-2-RE 41-6178 through 41-6305
P-47C-5-RE 41-6306 through 41-6667
P-47D-1-RE 42-7853 through 42-7957
P-47D-2-RE 42-7958 through 42-8402
P-47D-5-RE 42-8403 through 42-8702
P-47D-6-RE 42-74615 through 42-74964
P-47D-20-RE 42-25274 through 42-25322
P-47D-21-RE 42-25323 through 42-25538
P-47D-22-RE 42-25539 through 42-26388
P-47D-25-RE 42-26389 through 42-26773
P-47D-27-RE 42-26774 through 42-27384
P-47D-10-RE 42-74965 through 42-75214
P-47D-11-RE 42-75215 through 42-75614
P-47D-15-RE 42-75615 through 42-75864
P-47D-16-RE 42-75865 through 42-76118
P-47D-15-RE 42-76119 through 42-76364
P-47D-20-RE 42-76365 through 42-76613
P-47D-28-RE 44-19558 through 44-10307
P-47D-30-RE 44-20308 through 44-21107
P-47D-1-RA 42-22250 through 42-22363
P-47D-2-RA 42-22364 through 42-22563
P-47D-3-RA 42-22564 through 42-22663
P-47D-4-RA 42-22664 through 42-22863
P-47D-11-RA 42-22864 through 42-23113
P-47D-15-RA 42-23143 through 42-23299
P-47D-16-RA 42-23114 through 42-23142
P-47D-20-RA 43-25254 through 43-25440
P-47D-21-RA 43-25441 through 43-25664
P-47D-23-RA 43-25665 through 43-25753
P-47D-25-RA 42-27389 through 42-28188
P-47D-26-RA 42-28189 through 42-28438
P-47D-28-RA 42-28439 through 42-29466
P-47D-30-RA 44-32668 through 44-33867
P-47D-35-RA 44-89684 through 44-90283
P-47D-40-RA 44-90284 through 44-90483
P-47D-30-RA 45-49090 through 45-49554
XP-47F-RE 41-5938
XP-47E-RE 41-6065
P-47G-CU 42-24920 through 42-24939
P-47G-1-CU 42-24940 through 42-24979

P-47G-5-CU 42-24980 through 42-25039
P-47G-10-CU 42-25040 through 42-25119
P-47G-15-CU 42-25120 through 42-25273
XP-47H-RE 42-23297 and 42-23298
XP-47J-RE 43-46952
XP-47K-RE 42-8702
XP-47L-RE 42-76614
YP-47M-RE 42-27385 and 42-27386, 42-27388
P-47M-RE 44-21108 through 44-21237
XP-47N-RE 42-27387
P-47N-1-RE 44-87784 through 44-88333
P-47N-5-RE 44-88334 through 44-88883
    88883
P-47N-15-RE 44-88884 through 44-89083
P-47N-20-RE 44-89084 through 44-89283
P-47N-25-RE 44-89284 through 44-89450
P-47N-RE 44-89451 through 44-89683
    (cancelled)
P-47N-20-RA 45-49975 through 45-50123
P-47N-RA 45-50124 through 45-55174
    (cancelled)

Royal Air Force Serial Numbers

Mk I FL731 through FL850, HB962 through HB999, HD100 through HD181

Mk II HD182 through HD301, KJ128 through KJ367, KL168 through KL347, KL838 through KL887, and KL888 through KL976 which were cancelled

USSR Serial Numbers*

P-47D-10-RE 42-75201 through 42-75203
P-47D-22-RE 42-25539 through 42-25658
P-47D-27-RE 42-27015 through 42-27064, 42-27115 through 42-27164

*seven lost during delivery

RIGHT *Unusual formation of Tiger Destefani in the P-47D, Steve Barber in the Confederate Air Force's Grumman F8F-2 Bearcat N7825C and Robert Converse in the P-51D*

THUNDERBOLT SPECIFICATIONS

XP-47B

Span 40 ft 9 in
Length 35 ft
Height 12 ft 8 in
Wing Area 300 sq ft
Empty Weight 9189 lb
Loaded Weight 12,700 lb
Max Speed 412 mph
Ceiling 38,000 ft
Rate of Climb 3000 fpm
Range 575 mph
Powerplant P& W XR-2800-21 of 2000 hp

P-47B

Span 40 ft 9 in
Length 35 ft
Height 12 ft 8 in
Wing Area 300 sq ft
Empty Weight 9346 lb
Loaded Weight 13,360 lb
Max Speed 429 mph
Cruise Speed 340 mph
Ceiling 42,000 ft
Rate of Climb 2560 fpm
Range 550 miles
Powerplant P&W R-2800-21 of 2000 hp

P-47C

Span 40 ft 9 in
Length 35 ft
Height 14 ft 2 in
Wing Area 300 sq ft
Empty Weight 9900 lb
Loaded Weight 14,925 lb
Max Speed 433 mph
Cruise Speed 350 mph
Ceiling 42,000 ft
Rate of Climb 2400 fpm
Range 550 miles
Powerplant P&W R-2800-21 of 2000 hp

P-47D-30

Span 40 ft 9 in
Length 36 ft 1 in
Height 14 ft 2 in
Wing Area 300 sq ft
Empty Weight 10,000 lb
Loaded Weight 19,400 lb
Max Speed 428 mph
Cruise Speed 350 mph
Ceiling 42,000 ft
Rate of Climb 2200 fpm
Range 475 miles
Powerplant P&W R-2800-59 of 2300 hp

XP-47H

Span 40 ft 9 in
Length 39 ft 2 in
Height 14 ft 2 in
Wing Area 300 sq ft
Empty Weight 11,442 lb
Loaded Weight 13,750 lb
Max Speed 490 mph
Range 700 miles
Powerplant Chrysler XIV-2220-1 of 2300 hp

XP-47J

Span 40 ft 11 in
Length 33 ft 3 in
Height 17 ft 3 in
Wing Area 300 sq ft
Empty Weight 9663 lb
Loaded Weight 16,780 lb
Max Speed 507 mph
Cruise Speed 400 mph
Ceiling 45,000 ft
Rate of Climb 3100 fpm
Range 765 miles
Powerplant P&W R-2800-57 of 2800 hp

P-47M

Span 40 ft 9 in
Length 36 ft 4 in
Height 14 ft 9 in
Wing Area 308 sq ft
Empty Weight 10,423 lb
Loaded Weight 15,500 lb
Max Speed 473 mph
Ceiling 41,000 ft
Rate of Climb 3200 fpm
Range 530 miles
Powerplant P&W R-2800-57 of 2800 hp

P-47N

Span 42 ft 7 in
Length 36 ft 1 in
Height 14 ft 8 in
Wing Area 322 sq ft
Empty Weight 11,000 lb
Loaded Weight 20,700 lb
Max Speed 467 mph
Cruise Speed 300 mph
Ceiling 43,000 ft
Rate of Climb 3000 fpm
Range 800 miles
Powerplant P&W R-2800-57, -73, or -77 of
    2800 hp